PSALMS
1–72

Text copyright © Donald Coggan 1998

The author asserts the moral right
to be identified as the author of this work

Published by
The Bible Reading Fellowship
Sandy Lane West, Oxford, England
ISBN 1 84101 031 6

First edition 1998
10 9 8 7 6 5 4 3 2 1 0

Acknowledgments
The Revised English Bible © Oxford University Press and Cambridge
University Press, 1989
'I love you, O Lord, you alone' © Christopher Idle/Jubilate Hymns
Material from *The Alternative Service Book 1980* is copyright © The Central
Board of Finance of the Church of England and is reproduced by permission.
Extract from *Contemporary Parish Prayers* by Frank Colquhoun reproduced by
permission of Hodder and Stoughton Limited.
'Great is thy faithfulness' by William Runyan (1870–1957)/Thomas O.
Chisholm (1866–1960) copyright © 1951 Hope Publishing. Administered by
CopyCare, P.O. Box 77, Hailsham BN27 3EF Uk. Used by permission.
Excerpts from *Guerrillas of Grace: Prayers for the Battle* by Ted Loder, copyright
© 1984. Reprinted by permission of Innisfree Press, Philadelphia, PA.
Extracts from the Book of Common Prayer of 1662, the rights in which are
invested in the Crown in perpetuity within the United Kingdom, are
reproduced by permission of the Crown's patentee, Cambridge University
Press.
'Vespers' from *When We Were Very Young* by A.A. Milne, published by Methuen
Children's Books (a division of Egmont Children's Books Limited)
Extract by Rudyard Kipling courtesy of A.P. Watt Ltd on behalf of the National
Trust for Places of Historic Interest or Natural Beauty.

A catalogue record for this book is available
from the British Library

Printed and bound in Great Britain by Caledonian Manufacturing
International, Glasgow

PSALMS 1 – 72

THE PEOPLE'S BIBLE COMMENTARY

DONALD COGGAN

A BIBLE COMMENTARY FOR EVERY DAY

The Bible Reading Fellowship
OPENING THE BIBLE

EDITORS' FOREWORD

When this series of books was first planned, it was described as a Bible commentary that would speak to 'heart and mind'. Obviously readers need help with understanding and interpreting the text of the Bible, but our hope was that these books would also have as a central aim the *application* of the Bible's message. 'The word of God is living and active... able to judge the thoughts and intentions of the heart,' says the writer to the Hebrews. If the scriptures are in any meaningful sense the 'word of the Lord' then they are more than simply 'books', and they are there not just to be studied and interpreted, but applied to our lives.

When we invited Lord Coggan to contribute to the volumes on the Psalms, we had this aspect of the series very much in mind. As a distinguished Hebrew scholar, and chairman of the joint committee that produced the Revised English Bible, he was eminently qualified to explain and interpret the text of the Psalter. But as one of the great preachers of our time, he would, we felt, also be able to capture the passion and feeling of these remarkable writings and help his readers respond to them with 'heart' as well as 'mind'.

After all the Psalms are not prose, but *poetry*, and poetry requires a quite different approach from historical, narrative or didactic writings. If we miss the 'feel' of a psalm, then we miss its meaning too. In considering these poems, then, questions of authorship and text are interesting, but not as crucial as they may be in other scriptures. Consequently, while they are not ignored, the emphasis in this commentary is on meaning and message.

Two hundred years ago Matthew Henry said of the Psalms that 'none ever comes up so dry from David's well'. This commentary, by one who has known, loved and preached the Psalms all his life, will help us to dip eagerly into that deep and refreshing source.

The Editors

INTRODUCING
THE PEOPLE'S BIBLE COMMENTARY
SERIES

Congratulations! You are embarking on a voyage of discovery—or rediscovery. You may feel you know the Bible very well; you may never have turned its pages before. You may be looking for a fresh way of approaching daily Bible study; you may be searching for useful insights to share in a study group or from a pulpit.

The People's Bible Commentary (PBC) series is designed for all those who want to study the scriptures in a way that will warm the heart as well as instructing the mind. To help you, the series distils the best of scholarly insights into the straightforward language and devotional emphasis of Bible reading notes. Explanation of background material, and discussion of the original Greek and Hebrew, will always aim to be brief.

- If you have never really studied the Bible before, the series offers a serious yet accessible way in.

- If you help to lead a church study group, or are otherwise involved in regular preaching and teaching, you can find invaluable 'snapshots' of a Bible passage through the PBC approach.

- If you are a church worker or minister, burned out on the Bible, this series could help you recover the wonder of scripture.

Using a People's Bible Commentary

The series is designed for use alongside any version of the Bible. You may have your own favourite translation, but you might like to consider trying a different one in order to gain fresh perspectives on familiar passages.

Many Bible translations come in a range of editions, including study and reference editions that have concordances, various kinds of special index, maps and marginal notes. These can all prove helpful in studying the relevant passage. The Notes section at the back of each PBC volume provides space for you to write personal reflections, points to follow up, questions and comments.

Each People's Bible Commentary can be used on a daily basis, instead of Bible reading notes. Alternatively, it can be read straight through, or used as a resource book for insight into particular verses of the biblical book.

If you have enjoyed using this commentary and would like to progress further in Bible study, you will find details of other volumes in the series listed at the back, together with information about a special offer from BRF.

While it is important to deepen understanding of a given passage, this series always aims to engage both heart and mind in the study of the Bible. The scriptures point to our Lord himself and our task is to use them to build our relationship with him. When we read, let us do so prayerfully, slowly, reverently, expecting him to speak to our hearts.

Contents

Acknowledgments

I am grateful to Mrs Armorel Willmot for her patience in typing my manuscript and to the staff of the Bible Reading Fellowship for their skill in setting out the material.

PBC Psalms 1—72: Introduction

Sandals Off!

To open the book of Psalms is to find ourselves confronted by a mystery. The mystery is the fact of their appeal to people of all kinds, and their impact on them irrespective of time or circumstances. Let me illustrate. I begin with the testimony of a young man, a Cambridge graduate, a businessman with very bright prospects in the City of London. He gave it all up to go to Chile to work among the youth of that country and especially among the deprived. At the age of twenty-seven, he wrote to his parents:

My life has been transformed through the discovery of the voice of Christ in Scripture. Indeed, through learning to pray with the Bible a whole new world has opened up before me; where Life and Love are not defined by what suits me or society around me, but by that immeasurable power and presence we call God; and that God calls us to live that love in my own special vocation... I had never before really seen the Bible as a place to meet God... Yet... I found myself consuming the passion and yearning of the psalms that seems to reach across the centuries in my own increasingly desperate desire to know where and who God is. 'As a deer yearns for running streams so my soul is yearning for you, my God.'

Some sixteen centuries before this, Augustine of Hippo wrote about his experience as a young man when he read the psalms:

My God, how I cried to you when I read the Psalms of David, songs of faith, utterances of devotion which allow no pride of spirit to enter in! I was but a beginner in authentic love of you... How I cried out to you in those Psalms, and how they kindled my love for you! I was fired by an enthusiasm to recite them, were it possible, to the entire world in protest against the pride of the human race. Yet they are being sung in all the world—'there is none who can hide himself from your heat'. (Confessions)

Dr Allen Wicks, organist and choirmaster of Canterbury Cathedral from 1961 to 1988, has written of 'the tempestuous exhilaration of the psalmists' response to God':

At Canterbury my youthful admiration of the psalms became a passion, fed by the choristers' enthusiasm for these, by turns, trembling, angry, beseeching, challenging, fiery, trusting, accepting, radiant songs directed at Jehovah.

For myself, I have been fairly well acquainted with the psalms since I was a boy. But the writing of this book has brought me into a new relationship with them and, if I may dare say so, with their writers, and, I would hope, with their God and mine. For to understand a psalm, it is necessary to realize that we are treading on holy ground— where the saints have trod down long centuries. Early in his life, Moses came to Horeb, the mountain of God. There he saw the burning bush which was not burnt up. There God spoke to him: 'Do not come near! Take off your sandals, for the place where you are standing is holy ground' (Exodus 3:1–6). To enter into the meaning of the psalms we must take off our sandals. These writers were in touch with the Holy One. Sometimes they raged at him. Sometimes they adored him. Often they consciously did neither, but just got on with living a godly life *with an eye Godwards*. Sometimes they prayed alone, yet not alone, for God was with them. Often they prayed in the company of other faithful souls, in the great services of temple worship or in the less awesome surroundings of the synagogue. But it is 'sandals off!' if the secrets of the psalmists are to be disclosed. We are in touch with the God of Abraham, Isaac and Jacob, with the God and Father of our Lord Jesus Christ (for he used these psalms and made them his own). We are in touch with the spiritual resources of the saints of the ages.

Imagination is needed if the psalms are to release their treasures to us. It is hard to realize how different was the world of the psalmists from our world. Theirs was a world of few books and no phones, e-mail, or TV screens; a pastoral world, not one of tower-blocks and concrete; a world of flocks and cattle, not of investments; a world of country paths, not of macadamized streets; a tiny world far removed from any concept of travel in space, of light-years or of evolutionary processes. It might be thought that anything they wrote, or any poems which they handed down from generation to generation, would be so far removed from us as to be almost wholly worthless. But this is not so, and the reason is not far to seek. These ancient writers share with us a common humanity, and their writings touch our hearts and minds precisely because they deal with matters which most deeply affect us as human beings. Justice in a world where injustice reigns; relationships with God, with one another, with foreigners, with wicked people; love and hate; sickness and depression; sin and forgiveness—these are the stuff of which our humanity is made. These are the problems that torture us and tease us, whether we live in the year 2000BC or AD2000. Basically, we and the psalmists are one.

With sandals off, then, and imagination at the ready, you begin to read a psalm. Don't look for logic. The writer is not a scientist, at pains to watch every syllable he writes lest he get a fact wrong. Here are people in agony. Here are people exuberant. Here are people at moments of high spiritual experience. Don't look for logic. Rather, listen for a heartbeat. And remember that you are in the world of poetry—these psalms are *poems*, and poems need *time*...

This raises a matter of importance in the use of this book. Please do not try to 'do' one psalm a day. In the *New Daylight* Bible reading notes of the Bible Reading Fellowship, there is a brief passage of scripture and a comment for one day—and we move on to the next. This is not the purpose of these two volumes on the Psalms. I hope you will work your way through them, but not that you will finish in 150 days! You will notice that some comments are longer than others. I had to linger on one psalm before I went on to the next. I hope you will do the same. If a psalm is meeting your need or challenging your assumptions, stay with it, take your time with it. Chew the cud. 'Let yourself be filled' by a psalm or by a verse or a phrase in it. Meditate on it. Let it keep you company through a day, or even in the hours of a sleepless night, or on a walk. To use a phrase of the Chief Rabbi Jonathan Sacks: 'Create a space for the Shekinah' (God's presence).

The one and the many

There is an extraordinary intimacy which marks many of the psalms—the intimacy of a person's relationship with the Holy One. We notice it, for example in Psalm 18:1, when we see in our mind's eye a frail mortal looking up into the face of the Almighty and saying: 'I love you, Lord.' Or again in Psalm 42:1–2, when the psalmist says: 'As a hind longs for the running streams, so I long for you, my God. I thirst for God...' Or again, there is intimacy, the intimacy of a *break* of relationship and a sense of dereliction, when the psalmist cries out: 'My God, my God, why have you forsaken me?' (Psalm 22:1). By way of contrast, we look at the opening verses of Psalm 103, and find the psalmist calling on himself to 'bless the Lord' who has so blessed him, in pardoning him, healing him, rescuing him, satisfying him. In Psalm 34:8 he bids people share the satisfaction which he himself has found in God—'taste and see that the Lord is good'.

These writers are in touch with the living God. Each writer can only tell the world how it is with *him*. How can a couple, head over heels in love, convey their experience to their friends? When they attempt to do so, they can only stutter, or write a poem, or sing a song...

We cannot begin to express our relationship with God without the use of personal pronouns—he... me... What a revelation it was when Saul of Tarsus came to realize that 'the Son of God... loved *me* and gave himself up for *me*' (Galatians 2:20)! When Augustine pondered on the power of his mother's prayers in leading him out of the clutches of his old life into one made new in Christ, he said to God: 'You are good and all-powerful, *caring for each one of us as though the only one in your care*' (*Confessions* III.xi.19).

God, who is love, takes the initiative. A human being responds, sometimes very haltingly, but contact is made. That is where intimacy can be found, and the psalms are full of it.

But there is another element in the psalms, equally strong, equally pervasive. It is the sense of community. Religion for those writers is not 'the flight of the alone to the Alone'. Far from it. They write from the perspective of people who are what they are precisely because they are members of a nation which believes itself to have a special relationship with God. He has created this nation, revealed himself to it, called it, stayed with it in all its sufferings, sent it on his mission to the world. The psalmists write as members of the people of God.

The people had received a Law, a teaching, which they were not only committed to obey and live by, but of which they were also trustees. The figure of Moses towers over the writings of the Old Testament. Obedience to the Law that was given on Sinai led to prosperity (in the fulness of that word's meaning). Disobedience led to death and disaster. To receive that teaching and to pass it on faithfully was not the road to bondage or sterility. Rather, the reverse. Hence the note of joy and privilege which characterizes such a psalm as 119: 'In your commandments I find continuing delight; I love them with all my heart' (v. 47).

The psalms are the writings of members of a nation that was unique—unique in its sense of trusteeship, not in the sense of perfection. The story of Israel, the people of God, is one marred by constant failure, disobedience, contamination from polytheistic neighbours. But always there was a remnant which was loyal and through whom God would work out his purposes. The community might be small. Its purpose never changed.

The outstanding mark of this people of God was that it was a *worshipping* community. During the long weary years of wandering in the wilderness, the focus of their worship was the Tent of Meeting, marked by the pillar of cloud by day and of fire by night (see notes on Psalm 15). There God met with his people (see Exodus 25). There they learned the lessons of awe-full worship. When at last they settled in the land which God had promised them, tent worship gave way to temple worship. The first temple having been destroyed around 586BC, the building of the second temple was undertaken some six decades later. The prophecies of Haggai and Zechariah in which these men urged the work forward make interesting reading. In 167BC Antiochus Epiphanes desecrated the temple by offering a pig on its altar. Judas Maccabaeus, with enormous courage, supervised its re-dedication in 164BC, and the reconstruction of this magnificent building, supported by Herod the Great, was still in process when Jesus taught in its courts during his ministry.

Here the sacrifice of vast numbers of sheep and cattle went on in ceaseless succession. Here the tribes of the Lord went up to worship at the great feasts. Here music of all kinds accompanied the songs of the worshippers (see, for example, Psalm 150:3–6). The book of Psalms, much as we now have it, has justifiably been called 'the hymn-book of the second temple'. Its title in Hebrew is simply 'Praises'. No wonder that Jerusalem, the city where all this took place, has, from that day to this, evoked the deepest and most passionate feelings of love and loyalty. This was 'the city of God, the holy dwelling of the Most High; God is in her midst...' (Psalm 46:4, 5). 'His holy mountain is fair and lofty, the joy of the whole earth. The mountain of Zion... is the city of the great King' (Psalm 48:1, 2). 'Lord of Hosts,' cried one worshipper, 'how dearly loved is your dwelling place! I pine and faint with longing for the courts of the Lord's temple; my whole being cries out with joy to the living God' (Psalm 84:1, 2). 'I rejoiced,' said another worshipper, 'when they said to me, "Let us go to the house of the Lord". Now our feet are standing within your gates, Jerusalem: Jerusalem, a city built compactly and solidly' (Psalm 122:1–3).

The sheer solidity of the building with its massive stones spoke of the solidity of the promises of the God who entered into a covenant relationship with his people; the beauty of its construction and adornment, its golden doors shimmering in the light of the rising sun, spoke of his majesty and grace. One greater than any of the prophets, as he entered the city which had rejected him, God's supreme ambassador, broke down and wept: 'O Jerusalem, Jerusalem… how often have I longed to gather your children… but you would not let me' (Luke 13:34).

Worship, joyful worship, musical worship, corporate worship was at the centre of the life of the people of God; worship which led to upright and godly living. 'Lord, who may lodge in your tent? Who may dwell on your holy mountain? One of blameless life…' (Psalm 15:1, 2). In reading the psalms we learn much about the warmth and dynamism of Jewish worship and, if we have ears to hear, about Israel's God, creator, redeemer, King.

Text and authorship

If you compare the text of the Revised English Bible, which we are using, with that of the Authorized Version (1611) or the Prayer Book Version, you will notice very considerable differences in the translation. A good example would be Psalm 87. Why is this? Because in the passing down of this psalm, as indeed in many of them, the work of copying by hand has necessarily involved errors. Scholars have faced these difficulties, and given the best translations that they can, often making sense of a verse which in earlier versions made little or no sense at all.

It must be borne in mind that this book is not a verse-by-verse commentary. A series of volumes would be needed for that purpose—and there are many already on the scholars' shelves. Here we have often been bound to leave puzzling words or phrases without comment—that is regrettable but unavoidable. I have tried to convey the general 'feel' of the psalm and of the person who wrote it—to look at the poem through the eyes of the poet, and to get to the heart of its permanent message. If this leaves the reader to search in the commentaries for light on the details, so much the better.

'The person who wrote it... the eyes of the poet'. Who did write these psalms? Whose were the eyes of the poets? These are questions which admit of no easy answers. 'The Psalms of David' will not do, for clearly in the Psalter (the psalms as we now have them) we have a collection of poems by a wide variety of people. The headings of the psalms are not part of the original poems—they were added later. Some of them are headed 'for David', or it might be 'by David'. Some headings link the poem with some particular incident in David's career. Psalm 51 is a case in point, linking as it does David's adultery with Bathsheba (see 2 Samuel 11 and 12) with his broken-hearted penitence. That link adds special point both to the incident and to the psalm. 'The sweet Psalmist of Israel' (2 Samuel 23:1, Authorized Version), 'the singer of Israel's psalms' (Revised English Bible) may well have been the author of the psalms as well as the singer or accompanist of them.

What is clear is that we have in the collection a hymn-book of the people of God. As we read or chant these psalms we see a people at worship, communities of faith in the one and only God, at grips with him while being (many of them) surrounded by worshippers of wood and stone, holding on to their faith against all the odds of polytheistic counter-attractions. A collection, in the nature of the case, takes many years to come together; we have in these one hundred and fifty poems works from many centuries of Israel's experience—hence the rich mixture of despair and hope, of complaint and praise. The whole gamut of a nation's experience is reflected here, as well as a wide range of the joys and agonies of individuals.

Many of the psalms are intended to be set to music—hence the rich variety of instruments mentioned in them (see, for example, 150:3–5). The oft-recurring *Hallelujah* is probably a direction to the congregation to take its vocal part. And the word *lamenasseah* in the headings of some psalms, though its meaning is obscure, was very likely a musical direction. So the word *selah*, which is printed in the body of the text of many psalms, was probably a direction to the choir or musicians to 'strike up' (for example, in 3:2, 4).

The Psalter is divided into five books: 1—41; 42—72; 73—89; 90—106; 107—150). In this volume we consider the first two books (Psalms 1—72), reserving the other three for a second volume (Psalms 73—150).

There are two instances of duplication within the Psalter: Psalm 14 and Psalm 53 are virtually identical. Likewise, Psalm 40:13–17 is repeated almost word for word in Psalm 70. Such duplication may suggest that the five books of psalms may have been used separately, by different communities, and were later brought together to form the Psalter as we know it. I have chosen to consider Psalm 14 together with Psalm 53.

There is a wide variety of types in the Psalter as it has come down to us. There are psalms of complaint or lament, which are wrung from the heart of the writer as he thinks of his distress, sin or sickness (for example, 22; 38; 42—43). There are psalms of praise and exhilaration, songs of Zion, confident in the presence of the Lord in Jerusalem (for example, 46; 84; 122). There are royal psalms which celebrate the king as God's regent (for example, 2; 20; 45; 72). There are enthronement psalms in which the kingship of God is dwelt on (for example, 47; 93; 95—99). There are wisdom psalms which remind us of the book of Proverbs and (in the Apocrypha) the book of Wisdom (for example 34; 37). Some psalms are obviously for individual use, some for corporate worship. This should be borne in mind as each psalm is studied.

The authors of the psalms delighted in the use of parallelism, that is to say, the second part of the verse virtually repeats the first in order to underline it, deepen it or elaborate it. Or the second part of the verse may serve to make a contrast with the first, as in 1:6:

> *The Lord watches over the way of the righteous,*
> *but the way of the wicked is doomed.*

Some of the psalms are *acrostic*, with each verse or section beginning with a different letter of the Hebrew alphabet, the most elaborate being 119, with eight verses for each of the twenty-two letters of the Hebrew alphabet—quite a feat!

All these things (and a dozen others on which we have no space to comment) add interest to the poems we are about to study. But they are trivial compared with this point which we must always bear in mind: the value of the psalms lies in the fact that they face us constantly with the great major concepts which are Israel's distinctive gift to the world and for which we Christians are in everlasting debt to Israel—the righteousness of God; the loving compassion of God; the covenant-relationship between God and his people; the Law (teaching) of God; the yearning of the human heart for God; his yearning for us.

Imprecatory psalms

A special note is called for on the so-called imprecatory or cursing psalms.

At various points in this book we shall come across psalms, or parts of psalms, which are called 'imprecatory' or 'cursing' (for example, 58; 68:21–23; 69:22–28; 109:8–20; 137:7–9). I have thought it best to mention them here, rather than repeatedly comment on them as they occur.

In many prayerbooks they are bracketed as being unsuitable for use in public worship. There is much to be said for this. In the course of public worship they cannot be commented on, and their recitation only occasions offence or even revulsion on the part of those who are genuinely seeking to worship God.

But they are part and parcel of these poems, and it will not do simply to put our (mental) pen through the offending psalms and, by omitting them, to say in effect: 'We know better than the psalmists did. Did not Jesus say "Love your enemies and pray for your persecutors" (Matthew 5:44), and did not Paul say "My dear friends, do not seek revenge…" (Romans 12:19)? These passages are regrettable. Forget them!' We must go deeper than this.

It is not correct to describe these psalms as cursing psalms. The psalmists do not curse their enemies—they call on God to deal with the persons who have offended. They lament in passionate terms. They petition God. To transfer the vengeance which they feel on to God is to renounce their own vengeance, and that could be a cathartic experience for them.

Two positive points must be made. The first about the situation in which the psalmists found themselves and which gave rise to such violent reaction; the second about the character of the God to whom they address their prayers.

Firstly, we need to remember that the background of these psalms is not one of monastic or domestic calm, but one of extreme violence. The writers have reached a point of endurance beyond which they cannot go. No conventional means of justice is adequate for the situation in which they find themselves. Theirs is a violent age, and they or their loved ones are the victims of that violence. This is not difficult for us to appreciate today. We live in an age of violence. We see that violence wreaked on innocent children—raped, abused, hit by drunken drivers... We read the comments of their parents: 'May they burn in hell for ever'. Conventional churchgoers are shocked by such reactions. But is there not in all of us some measure of fellow-feeling?

The psalmists are passionate people. They feel, and they put their feelings into words. But they know where to turn *in extremis*. They turn to God. They are driven to the Holy One. Let him deal with the situation—vengeance is *his* concern! They pray, and their prayer may not be much better than an angry blurt. But at the end, they can sing—or most of them can!

Secondly, we must reflect on what sort of God it is that they pray to. What is his character? He is a God who is concerned about real-life situations. His name is Yahweh ('I am what I am' or 'I will be what I will be'). He will make himself known by what he does. He is the Just One who is concerned for human justice. He is grieved about his creation when it goes wrong, about his creatures when his image in them is defaced and they 'come short of the glory of the Lord' (Romans 3:23). A place must be left for divine retribution (Romans 12:19).

Imagine yourself in a situation like that of the psalmists. You have been deeply injured, offended, hurt. What courses of action are open to you? On the one hand, you can internalize your feelings—'let them burn in hell'. But if you do that, the odds are that you will damage yourself more than you will damage them. You will remain bitter, and you will be nervously and quite possibly physically damaged. On the other hand, you can externalize your feelings. You can tell God not only what you feel but also what you would do if you were in control of the situation. Get it off your chest. Tell him—if that is how you feel—that you would congratulate the person who seized their babes and dashed them against a rock (Psalm 137:9). Ask God to act—and leave the timing to him. Your language, when you come back later to look at it, may have been revolting, shocking. But God's back is strong enough to bear it and to deal with it. The God in whose hands you have decided to leave things is the Judge. But he is also the Saviour. His judgment, fearful though it is, is creative. His reaction to sin is not to be thought of in terms of offended dignity, but rather of outraged love.

I am conscious that this introduction leaves many questions unanswered. But at least it offers an approach which takes the problem seriously and deserves following up.

In this book, I do not refer readers to many books on the psalms. I want them to study the psalms themselves, the text being open before them. Commentaries can wait. But in the context of the imprecatory psalms I mention two books which I have found helpful: Walter Brueggemann's *Praying the Psalms* (St Mary's Press, Christian Book Publications) and Eric Zenger's *A God of Vengeance. Understanding the Psalms of Divine Wrath* (Westminster/John Knox Press). In commenting on a few of the psalms (Psalms 22, 31, 42 and 43), I have also drawn on material from my book *The Voice from the Cross* (Triangle), a meditation on the seven words of Jesus.

Donald Coggan

PSALM 1

The WAY *of* DELIGHT

We begin our study of the psalms on a happy note, an exclamation
of delight, literally 'oh, the happinesses of the one who… !' A living
faith in God does not lead to the production of kill-joys. The reverse
is the case. 'The harvest of the Spirit is… joy' (Galatians 5:22).
Perhaps this psalm is put first in the collection of 150 psalms because
it emphasizes the choice which faces us all: 'Make up your mind, it's
up to you.'

The first three verses sketch this happy person; then follows a
description of his opposite number. The concluding verse sums up
the two-fold picture.

Verse 1 suggests a definite rejection of a certain way of life which
destroys a person's character: 'Happy is the one who does not take
the counsel of the wicked for a guide.' This man has decided that the
'path', the way of life of the 'wicked', the 'sinners', the 'scoffers', is
not to be his way. He rejects the values of such people, their refusal
to put God at the centre of their lives. As he looks at them, the trivi-
ality of their lives strikes him—they are like *chaff* (v. 4), lightweight,
subject to every wind that blows, unstable. In a court of law (v. 5—
'when judgment comes'), they do not have a chance—anyone can
see through their hollowness.

Choosing friends

Look at this happy man. He chooses his companions with care. This
is not to suggest that he is a religious snob who despises those who
do not share his outlook. Of course he will mix with them, learn from
them, enjoy them. But you can tell a man by his friends. People of
faith need other men and women of faith with whom to share their
convictions, from whom to learn truths they have not yet discovered.
Christian growth is best nourished in the company of other believers.

This happy man watches his thought-life. He *delights* to meditate
on the things of God. If our minds are a cesspool, it is unlikely that
our actions will be noble. 'What you think, you are.' If he learns to
meditate daily—and sometimes in the watches of the night—on the
law of the Lord, he will keep fresh mentally and morally. The roots of
his character will go down into well-watered soil. There will be a light

in his eye and a spring in his step. Happy man!

This portrait is made the clearer because it is set against the dark background of the happy man's opposite number (vv. 4–5). The contrast is stark. There is judgment to come and only a fool will forget it.

Freedom from care

Verse 6 depicts the freedom from care we experience when we know that the Lord is watching our way: 'The Lord watches over the way of the righteous, but the way of the wicked is doomed.'

Let us take an example of this sense of freedom: Elizabeth has left school and is going off to college. She is a Christian. As such, she will not shut herself up in a kind of holy aloofness from her fellow students. On the contrary she will mix freely with them—in work, in games, in cultural pursuits. But she will not be ashamed of being seen, very frequently, in the company of those who put God first. In fact, in them she will find an intimacy which will deepen her discipleship and begin to make her a woman of God. Such intimacy, of friendship and prayer, will serve to keep out the damp fog of a way of life which, at its worst, scoffs at the things of God, or, more frequently, has no time for them at all.

The marks of the truly 'happy' person, as Jesus depicts them, can be found in the opening words of the Sermon on the Mount (Matthew 5:3–12). They are a fine elaboration of the psalmist's happy man. Such people are 'salt to the world' (Matthew 5:13), that is to say, by their presence they save society from going bad, and they add zest to life—and these are the main functions of salt. And they are 'light for all the world' (Matthew 5:14)—society minus Christian light is very dark!

PRAISE

Thanks be to God for his watchful care.

2

PSALM 2

GOD ENTHRONED

On first reading, this psalm looks difficult. To understand it we should read 2 Samuel 7:1–16. Here King David announces to Nathan the prophet his intention to build a temple for God. Through Nathan, God replies that David is not the man to do this. Rather, God will do something for him. God will build up the royal house of David. When David dies, his son will succeed him—Solomon will be the one to build the temple. God will establish his throne. God will be a father to him; he will be a son to God (v. 14)! That is something very special—a covenant-relationship between God and his people, focused in the person of the king. No wonder that, in such a psalm as this (and in, for example, Psalms 72 and 110), the emphasis on Israel's ruler-king-Messiah is so emphatic. The king is a person of very great importance, subservient only to God. Providing he acts righteously, his throne will be secure. Little Israel, surrounded by powerful nations themselves in turmoil (v. 1), has nothing to fear.

God sits enthroned above the nations (v. 4): 'I have enthroned my king (v. 6), my son (v. 7) on Zion, my holy mountain,' he says. It is the nations that should tremble, not Israel.

Bitter experiences

The violent language which the psalmist uses about God—laughing, deriding (v. 4), angrily rebuking, threatening (v. 5), striking down in mid-course, his anger flaring up (v. 11)—reflects, no doubt, the bitter experience of a nation which previously had suffered severely at the hands of invading powers. We shall have occasion later on to think about language which speaks of God in human terms, his anger, and so on (see on Psalm 7). Meanwhile we should do well to warn ourselves that when we speak of human anger, such a concept is often mixed with and marred by a constituent element in us of bad temper or irritability. When we speak of God, there is no such element. His wrath, his indignation, is pure.

In this, the first of the so-called royal psalms, the *character* of Israel's king is not indicated. In Psalm 72, however, it is spelled out in some detail, while Psalm 20 presents another aspect of kingship.

We can imagine this psalm being used in dramatic form at the enthronement of successive kings, and can hear the shouts of the people as they join in the ceremonies. With a righteous king established on the throne, the Israelites could go back to their homes, secure in the knowledge that God had his eye on king and people alike.

PRAISE

Happy are all who find refuge in him! (v. 12)

3

FAITH *in* DARK TIMES

Many psalms have superscriptions. This is the first: 'A psalm for David (when he fled from his son Absalom)'. They were not originally part of the psalms; they were added later. Some were musical directions, often obscure to us; others linked the psalm with particular historical events. Here the link with David's flight from his own son Absalom adds poignancy to the psalm. It is worth reading 2 Samuel 15:13–16 which recounts the story. Events reach their climax with David's moving lamentation on his son's tragic death (2 Samuel 18:33).

The language describing the psalmist's foes is general—they are numerous and godless: 'Lord, how numerous are my enemies! How many there are who rise against me, how many who say of me, "He will not find safety in God!"' (vv. 1 and 2); myriad are the forces ranged against him on every side (v. 6). But the scene is by no means entirely dark. The psalmist has a lively faith in God who is his 'shield' and his 'glory'. God answers his prayers: 'As often as I cry aloud to the Lord, he answers from his holy mountain' (v. 4). Ultimate victory is assured (v. 8).

Resting in God

There is no need, then, for stress and strain. With such a trust in God, the psalmist can sleep and wake refreshed, for he is upheld by God (v. 5). In the next psalm there is a similar reference to untroubled sleep, based on God's presence and care (Psalm 4:8). Another psalmist assures us that Israel's guardian 'never slumbers, never sleeps' (Psalm 121:4). With such a guardian, why fret or worry? Why toss and turn?

There is no easy overall recipe to cure sleeplessness. It brings distress to many who suffer from it, and its causes are many. But the National Health Service bill for sleeping-tablets would be greatly reduced if more people shared the psalmist's assurance of a guardian God, if more people formed the habit of saying to God as the last activity of the day: 'Into your hands, O Lord, I commend my spirit, for you have redeemed me, O God of truth' (Psalm 31:5).

Peter puts this well in his first letter: 'He cares for you, so cast all your anxiety on him' (1 Peter 5:7). A conscience at rest, a quiet confidence in God—these are treasures beyond all price or pills.

PRAYER

Save us, O Lord, while waking,
And guard us while sleeping,
that awake we may watch with Christ,
and asleep we may rest in peace.

Office of Compline

My heart is glad and my spirit rejoices,
my body too rests unafraid.

Psalm 16:9

4

PSALM 4

The SAVIOUR-GOD

God is addressed directly at the beginning and end of this psalm (vv. 1, 7, 8). The intervening verses (vv. 2–6) are addressed to 'men of rank'.

There is gratitude in this psalm. The writer is in touch with the God who answers his call and upholds his right (his cause). He is a Saviour-God—he has set him free when he was in a tight corner (v. 1) and has put in his heart a deep happiness (v. 7) which enables him to sleep well (v. 8a) and to live securely (v. 8b): 'Now in peace I shall lie down and sleep; for it is you alone, Lord, who let me live in safety.'

False gods

Who are these 'men of rank'? We do not know. Business associates, perhaps? They are a godless lot. They dishonour his glorious God and set their hearts on sham gods of their own (v. 2), lacking restraint, a noisy set who know nothing of meditative silence, sitting loose to the duties of religion (v. 5).

The objects of their worship are empty idols, false gods. We may take these words literally, for Israel was surrounded by nations where polytheism reigned, and it was all too easy to forsake God for other local deities. But it is pretty clear that the writer has in mind less tangible, but no less threatening, gods: the gods of materialism. Their worshippers get their happiness from successful business transactions and from 'living it up' with 'grain and wine in plenty' (v. 7). Look at their prayer (v. 6): it is a prayer for success, that God will smile on them and give them 'good times'. All they know about gratitude is worldly success. When everything is going their way, when they have won a cup at the races or at Wimbledon, they look up to heaven with a gesture of gratitude—and there's no more to it than that. When tragedy strikes, they are the first to ask, 'Why has God done this to me?'

The gods of a superficial religion, of materialism, are the favourite gods of the rich nations of Europe, of Japan, of America, of thousands of British institutions and homes. The psalmist's God is wholly different from these so-called gods. The happiness he gives does not depend on success as the world sees it (good crops, lucky invest-ments, a win in the Lottery). He is a God who answers prayer: 'the Lord hears when I call to him' (v. 3). He is a God who gives 'a greater happiness' (v. 7), a peace which passes understanding (v. 8), an inner serenity. Jesus was at pains to teach that 'even when someone has more than enough, his possessions do not give him *life*' (Luke 12:15).

PRAYER

O almighty God… grant unto thy people, that they may love the thing which thou commandest… that so… our hearts may surely there be fixed, where true joys are to be found; through Jesus Christ our Lord.

From the Collect of the Fourth Sunday after Easter, *Book of Common Prayer*

5

A MAN *of* PRAYER

It does not take much imagination to draw a mental picture of the person who wrote this psalm. There is much in it which calls for admiration. He is clearly a man of God, a man of prayer. He knows where to go when there is trouble afoot. In the morning (v. 3) he prepares his sacrifice and is off to God's house, the temple. It is God's love that draws him there; he can but bow down in awe (v. 7). His prayer is straightforward—'Lead me and protect me, Lord... give me a straight path to follow' (v. 8).

His concept of God is that of One who is essentially righteous, hating wickedness, abhorring violence and deceit (vv. 4–6).

The psalmist is in deep trouble. It looks as if his enemies are bringing false charges against him—'nothing they say is true'. Smooth in their talk, they beset him: 'they are bent on complete destruction. Their throats are gaping tombs' (v. 9b).

A vigorous reaction!

His reaction to these wicked men is, to say the least, vigorous! We shall often meet this kind of reaction in later psalms. Here are people who have got to a point beyond which their frail efforts are of no avail. They realize how precarious life is. They are at the edge of disaster. They are overwhelmed, nearly destroyed, but with enough life within them to cry out to the Holy One, to bring it all before him, their own desire for the destruction of their enemies included. This is no occasion for pious phraseology before God. The psalmist's fear and inadequacy make him spill it all out—I had almost said spit it all out—before God. Isn't this real religion? Why be namby-pamby when you feel mad with God and others?

He gets it all off his chest—and to his surprise finds that he can trust, even shout for joy, exult in God, and know that he will be surrounded with God's 'favour as with a shield' (vv. 11–12).

For MEDITATION

*It is a good way to start the day: 'I shall prepare a morning
sacrifice and keep watch' (v. 3). A few minutes spent every
morning in peaceful recollection and in commitment to God's will
and purposes are never wasted.*

*New every morning is the love
Our wakening and uprising prove;
Through sleep and darkness safely brought,
Restored to life and power and thought.*

*New mercies, each returning day,
Hover around us while we pray;
New perils past, new sins forgiven,
New thoughts of God, new hopes of heaven.*

John Keble (1792–1866)

6

PSALM 6

GOD'S ANGRY PUNISHMENT

In Psalm 5 we saw that it was *people* who were making trouble for the psalmist. He was beset by enemies who maligned him. In Psalm 6, apart from brief references to people who are workers of evil and apparently plague him (vv. 7b, 8, 10), it is sheer physical and perhaps nervous sickness which gets him down—his strength fails, his body is racked with pain, he is distraught (vv. 2, 3), he cannot sleep, he can only weep: 'I am wearied with my moaning; all night long my pillow is wet with tears, I drench the bed with my weeping. Grief dims my eyes; they are worn out because of all my adversaries' (vv. 6, 7).

Two things exacerbate his trouble. The first is that he thinks that his sickness is God's angry punishment for his sin (v. 1). The second is that he has little or no hope of anything worthwhile after death (v. 5).

Deep questions

Both of these things raise deep questions and will recur in later psalms. Here one comment on each may be helpful:

First, we may hold fast to the saying: 'God does not willingly afflict or punish any mortal' (Lamentations 3:33). We should be more than wary in saying, when confronted, for example, by the death of a child or young person, 'God willed it'. God allows it, and is certainly able to bring some good out of the tragedy. Sometimes, of course, we bring disaster on ourselves by our own folly (for example, the death by lung cancer of a heavy smoker). But the cry 'Why did God do this to me?', while entirely understandable, is to be treated with the greatest caution.

Second, 'among the dead no one remembers you; in Sheol who praises you?' (v. 5). *Sheol*, to the writers of the Old Testament, is the place of souls after death. It is 'the pit', the 'lower parts of the earth'. It is full of shades and darkness. It speaks of absence from God— there is no praising him there! People went *down* to it, mourning. Its bonds tighten around them (Psalm 18:5). Silence reigns.

A different picture

How Judaism later cast off this gloomy picture must not detain us here. The New Testament paints a very different picture: Jesus, by his rising, 'has broken the power of death and brought life and immortality to light through the gospel' (2 Timothy 1:10). 'Among the dead no one remembers you' (v. 5); to this the Christian replies 'one day we shall see face to face' (1 Corinthians 13:12). 'In Sheol who praises you?' (v. 5); to this the Christian replies 'a vast throng... standing before the throne and the Lamb... shouted aloud: "Victory to our God who sits on the throne, and to the Lamb!"' (Revelation 7:9, 10).

For MEDITATION

The poet William Cowper (1731–1800) was subject to attacks of depression. But he was a man of faith and he could write:

*Sometimes a light surprises
The Christian while he sings;
It is the Lord who rises
With healing in his wings;
When comforts are declining,
He grants the soul again
A season of clear shining
To cheer it after rain.*

*Though vine nor fig-tree neither
Their wonted fruit should bear,
Though all the fields should wither,
Nor flocks nor herds be there;
Yet, God the same abiding,
His praise shall tune my voice;
For, while in him confiding,
I cannot but rejoice.*

Nothing in all creation... can separate us from the love of God in Christ Jesus our Lord.

Romans 8:39

HIGHLY COLOURED WORDS

There are three *dramatis personae* in this highly coloured psalm—God, the writer's enemies, and the writer himself.

God is depicted as a refuge (v. 1), a shield (v. 10), there to rescue and save the man from his predicament; a righteous judge, searching human hearts and minds (v. 9), there to administer judgment on both individuals and nations: 'The Lord passes sentence on the nations. Uphold my cause, Lord, as my righteousness deserves, for I am clearly innocent.' 'God is a just judge, constant in his righteous anger' (vv. 8, 11).

The writer's enemies are described vividly and compared to a lion ready to kill and carry off the prey (v. 2), a warrior armed with a sharp sword (v. 12), an archer with his bow ready strung (v. 12), and a woman about to give birth—but all that appears is lies (v. 14)!

As far as the writer is concerned, the psalm is a protestation of his innocence, and a call on his God to recognize and vindicate that innocence. There is much in this psalm which reminds us of Job's protest—'a blameless and upright' man 'who feared God and set his face against wrongdoing' (Job 1:1) and yet was the victim of almost unbearable suffering.

God asleep?

Anthropomorphism means the attribution of human form or behaviour to God. We have many instances of it in the psalms and we might as well have a look at it now. 'God is spirit' (John 4:24). But we have bodies, and if we are to speak with any reality about God we can only do so if we use physical terms. Thus we speak of God's *eyes* being open (Psalm 11:4), his *arms* outstretched (Psalm 44:3), his *nostrils* emitting smoke (Psalm 18:8), and so on. Perhaps one of the most daring uses of such language is to speak of God as asleep. Sleep implies inactivity and inability to act. Sometimes, with great boldness and in extreme suffering, the psalmists charge God with being asleep—this would be blasphemous if it were not said by people in agony. We have an instance in this psalm—'Arise, Lord... rouse yourself... my God, *awake*' (v. 6). Even more peremptorily, another psalmist says, 'Rouse yourself, Lord; why do you sleep? Awake...'

(Psalm 44:23); and another even more daringly says, 'the Lord awoke as a sleeper wakes or a warrior flushed with wine' (Psalm 78:65).

There are risks in the use of such language, even by those whose hearts are well-nigh broken. But honesty with God is what matters, and he respects that in our dealings with him. Have you never reached the point at which, having prayed for long years for some good thing without any sign of divine response, you have said, 'Wake up, Lord'?

PRAYER

Teach us, Lord, the right mix of honesty with awe,
forthrightness with reverence.

SOVEREIGN LORD

This psalm begins and ends with identical words: 'Lord our sovereign, how glorious is your name throughout the world!' It is within this framework of adoration that the rest of the psalm is set. God in his majesty is praised in the vastness of the heavens and even babes and infants (v. 2) chip in! The God who elicits the praise of his universe is a God of justice, concerned for his creation, and concerned about those who flout his laws (v. 2b).

Starry heavens

Within that framework comes the main body of the psalm (vv. 3–8). In my mind I see a man in the desert, sleepless one night. He gives up trying to sleep and emerges from his tent. He sniffs the night air and fills his lungs. He looks up into the sky and gazes at the heavens, the moon and the stars which his God has set in place. He knows nothing of what scientists many years later will discover about the immensity of an expanding universe—telescopes are things of the far distant future. But even so, something of the vastness and mystery of the night sky dawns on him. Its blackness is dotted with points of light, seen with a clarity denied to those who live in cities. What he sees is enough to frighten him—there is a dreadful silence—no answering voice comes from the stars. How frail and transitory is humankind! How frail is his own little life—'what is a frail mortal?' (v. 4)—'what am I?'

We might expect that his answer to those questions would be 'a mere nothing, here today and gone tomorrow, a man in transit, with a life liable to be snuffed out at any moment, a breath…' The great God up there can hardly be expected to notice him. After all, he has a universe to run. How could he be expected to be mindful of him, or, for that matter, any of his fellows?

A listening God

The writer finds no such answer. In fact, he finds himself in a kind of conversation with God, a soliloquy, addressed half to himself and half to the God who, he is persuaded, is a listening God. The frail mortal is (he realizes) little less than a god, crowned with glory and honour, master over God's creation, ruler of the animal world—cattle, wild beasts, birds and fish (vv. 5–8).

Perhaps Shakespeare had this passage in mind when he wrote: 'What a piece of work is a man! how noble in reason! how infinite in faculty! in form, in moving, how express and admirable! in action how like an angel! in apprehension how like a god! the beauty of the world! the paragon of animals!' (*Hamlet*, Act 2 Scene 2). Such an estimate of the nature of humankind, taken by itself, could easily lead to *hubris*, arrogance—'I am the master of my fate: I am the captain of my soul'. Nothing is further from the psalmist's thought. It is *God* who has made humans like that—'*you* have made him little less than a god... *you* make him master...' (vv. 5, 6). So—men and women are God's vice-gerents, responsible to him and to him alone, answerable to him for the power he has put in their hands.

MEDITATION

Such a passage as this is the very foundation of a Christian ecology. This is why caring for the created world should occupy so prominent a place in any Christian ethic. Of this we shall see more in other psalms, for example Psalm 24:1. The earth is the Lord's. We are his stewards. We neglect this insight at our peril.

9 PSALMS 9 AND 10

GOD MOST HIGH

The themes of these two psalms aim to give a picture, so far as human words can ever dare to try, of a God Most High (v. 2), a God enthroned (vv. 4, 7, 11), a God who is a righteous Judge (vv. 4, 7, 8), who 'will try the cause of peoples with equity' (v. 8). This is a concept uncongenial to much modern thinking. It strikes a note rarely heard. It is a dimension of truth rarely emphasized. Before we dismiss it as an aspect of Old Testament religion which has been superseded, we had better note our Lord's parable of the sheep and goats in Matthew 25:31–46: the Son of Man sitting 'on his glorious throne, with all the nations gathered before him'.

The unjust world

Our first psalm is concerned with *personal* right and wrong—'my right and my cause' (v. 4). But the writer is more concerned with *nations*, with the ungodly (v. 5), the unjust world, the peoples (v. 8) who use their power to oppress the defenceless, the nations who are heedless of God (v. 17). God is concerned with the 'afflicted... he does not ignore their cry' (v. 12).

The sheer stupidity of such nations is held up for our scorn. Can they not see that when they dig a pit, it will be to their own undoing; when they cast a net to trap the helpless, they will themselves get entangled (v. 15)? 'Take away justice,' said Augustine, 'and what are kingdoms but mighty bands of robbers?' (*On the City of God*). When the wealthy nations of our modern world engage in the arms race and put vast resources into the making of landmines—our fair earth has 190 million of them hidden beneath its soil—do they ever stop to consider the frown on the face of a righteous God? The answer is—generally—'No'. There is a pitilessness to ungodliness which surpasses imagination.

'The wicked are trapped in their own devices' (v. 16)—they are to be found in the financial centres of the countries which invest in these abominations, in the laboratories which make them, in the battlefields of those who use them. Their future? 'Sheol' (v. 17), the place of darkness which the smile of God cannot illumine.

Individual wickedness

The writer of Psalm 10, when he is describing the ungodly and their activities, is less concerned with national problems and more with *individual* wickedness. He is impressed with their arrogance (vv. 2, 4, 6), the evil nature of their speech (v. 7), their animal cunning (vv. 8–10), their banishment of God from their thoughts: 'He says to himself, "God has forgotten; he has hidden his face and seen nothing"' (v. 11). It is a grim picture.

The writer of these two psalms is perplexed. Small wonder! Who of us is not perplexed when faced with the mystery of iniquity? There are times when God seems to be far off, seems to be hiding himself, seems to be inactive (Psalm 10:1, 12). The psalmist cries out for divine intervention—'break the power of the wicked' (v. 15). He finds it hard to see the wicked getting away with it. But there are shafts of light and of confidence in God, shouts of praise as faith breaks through—'I shall give praise to you, Lord' (Psalm 9:1–2); 'the Lord is King for ever and ever' (Psalm 10:16). God is listening and giving heed: 'Lord, you have heard the lament of the humble; you strengthen their hearts, you give heed to them' (Psalm 10:17).

Expressing liberation

Paul wrestles with the problem in his letters, especially in Romans 8. 'The whole created universe,' he writes, 'in all its parts groans as if in the pangs of childbirth' (v. 22). Nor is the Christian exempt from the pain and the perplexity—'we also, to whom the Spirit is given... are groaning' (v. 23). But with the groaning there is a sense of expectation... 'we look forward eagerly to... our liberation from mortality'. 'The universe itself is to be freed from the shackles of mortality and to enter upon the glorious liberty of the children of God' (v. 21). In Christ, 'God in all his fulness chose to dwell, and through him to reconcile all things to himself' (Colossians 1:19–20). His plan for the ultimate victory of good over evil stands for all time. Here is our hope.

PRAYER

Lord, make me an instrument of your peace.
Where there is hatred, let me sow love,
where there is despair, hope.

Attributed to Francis of Assisi

10 PSALM 11

UNDERMINING *the* FOUNDATIONS

In one brief sentence the writer tells us where he stands: 'In the Lord I take refuge.' 'Nonsense,' says someone, and proceeds to spell out his case. His speech occupies the second half of verse 1, all of verse 2, and I think probably verse 3. The Revised English Bible ends the inverted commas at the end of verse 2. But it may well be that verse 3 is part of the objector's case—'the foundations of your life and of your argument won't hold water—they are undermined; there's nothing that a man of God like you ("the just person") can do about it.'

The cynical voice from centuries before Christ has a very modern ring to it: 'the case for Christianity is untenable in a scientific age. The old beliefs are superseded by modern thought'. Often as not, these objections come from those who have never studied the claims of Christianity or of science, and base their objections on some half-baked travesties of the faith and outdated concepts of science given to them in their childhood. The media are not backward in forwarding such objections and in hampering those who stand for Christian truth and morals. The press is quick to take up cases of immorality, especially among the clergy, and if there is a sexual content to the case, so much the better for the press. They hint that the decline in church attendance is such that we may expect the funeral of the Church in the very near future. As to morals, why bother with the sayings of Jesus or the long traditions of the faith? A new day has dawned. The best course for the Christian is to 'flee like a bird to the mountains' (v. 1); the foundations are undermined and there's nothing to be done about it (v. 3). So—'the day of freedom has dawned. Let us eat and drink, for tomorrow we die. Join us on the slippery slope down the way to chaos'.

God reigns

The psalmist's reply (vv. 4–7) takes the form not of an argument but of a statement of conviction. There is a time and place for argument and debate, for being 'ready to make your defence when anyone challenges you to justify the hope which is in you' (1 Peter 3:15). But that time was not the right one for our psalmist. He simply faces his opponents with a declaration of things without which he cannot make any sense of life. God *reigns*—the throne of the universe is not empty (v. 4)—he reigns in his *temple* (so presumably worship matters). God *sees*—his searching eye tests humanity (v. 4). God *judges*: 'The Lord weighs just and unjust, and he hates all who love violence. He will rain fiery coals and brimstone on the wicked' (vv. 5, 6). God is *concerned* about social justice (v. 7). These are the things that abide. There are other things which, if neglected, lead to chaos and disaster. Is there the trace of an invitation in the second half of verse 7—'wouldn't you like to have God's smile on you?'

PRAYER

Let us pray for a right sense of timing: that God will show us when to state the case for our faith; and when, without a word, to let the witness of a holy life do its own work.

A BAD DAY

There is a note of bitterness about this psalmist—he is a disillusioned man. It looks to me as if he has been the victim of a raw deal—he has been let down with a thud. He looks around and sees that he is by no means alone in the experience. His bitterness is such that he indulges in a generalization: 'No one who is loyal remains; good faith between people has vanished' (v. 1). He has hit a bad day!

The disease of deceit

Nevertheless the writer has put his finger firmly on a disease which gnaws at the vitals of society—'smooth talk', duplicity, double-dealing, deceit, promising what you know you cannot produce just in order to win votes. Is not this the temptation which, yielded to, soils politics—'vote for me and all will be sunshine and roses'? In the advertising world, this is known as hype—we are surrounded by advertisements which lead the foolish up the garden path. We pay for the goods, only to find that they are spurious.

The power of the word, spoken, written, broadcast, is immense. We should read again the letter of James 3:5–12, and lay to heart the writer's vivid imagery—'the tongue is a fire...'

The duplicity of which our psalmist writes bears hardest on the poor and needy—they have nothing to cushion themselves against the plundering attacks. God is not unmindful of their plight: '"Now I will arise," says the Lord, "for the poor are plundered, the needy groan; I shall place them in the safety for which they long"' (vv. 5, 7).

A study in contrasts

This psalm is a study in contrasts—the smooth words of the deceivers and the unalloyed words of the Lord, like refined silver, or purified gold (v. 6). When God pronounces, he delivers. When he makes a covenant, he keeps his side of the bargain. As Paul puts it: 'All the promises of God have their Yes in Jesus Christ' (2 Corinthians 1:20).

Our society would be the cleaner if Christians complained less about those whose words influence public opinion, and prayed more for them. We should pray for those who represent us in the world of politics, culture, entertainment, drama... and for those who spread 'the words of the Lord' which are 'unalloyed' (v. 6)—for preachers, Bible translators and commentators.

PRAYER

We pray, Lord, for those who as writers, speakers and entertainers influence the thought of our people through the press, radio and television. Help them to exercise their gifts with responsibility and understanding, that they may enrich the common life of the nation and strengthen the forces of truth and goodness; through Jesus Christ our Lord.

Frank Colquhoun, *Contemporary Parish Prayers*

PSALM 13

CRYING OUT *to* GOD

'How long, Lord?' Four times in two verses the cry goes up. The psalmist is an anguished soul, there is a continuous grief in his heart. Within is agony; without an enemy lording it over him. No wonder he cries out to God.

There is no harm in such a prayer. We all utter it from time to time. God understands. We long for immediate answers, for quick resolution of our problems. But if we could see the situation through God's eyes, we might come to see that there are lessons to be learnt by delay. God's timing is perfect—his clock is never slow. Perhaps he wants to teach us about *endurance.*

Endurance is a big word in the language of the Bible. Here is the prophet Habakkuk—it would be worthwhile to turn to his little book. His prophecy begins with the cry, 'How long, Lord... ?' The whole of the first chapter is given to a description of wickedness run riot, justice perverted, international savagery, the triumph of wrong over right. He cries out to God, 'but you do not come to the rescue' (Habakkuk 1:2); 'Why... do you countenance the treachery of the wicked? Why keep silent when they devour those who are more righteous?' (v. 13). Is there no end to their pitilessness (v. 17)?

Habakkuk stops to take breath. What is God trying to teach him? He had better be on the look-out 'to hear what he says to me' (Habakkuk 2:1). The answer comes like the calm after a raging storm: 'There is still a vision for the appointed time... though it delays, wait for it, for it will surely come before too long' (Habakkuk 2:3). Habakkuk, stop your raging. Learn to wait and to listen. Learn the meaning of endurance and steadfastness.

Standing firm

Christ learned that hard lesson. Paul speaks of his steadfastness and prays that the Lord will 'direct your hearts towards... the steadfastness of Christ' (2 Thessalonians 3:5). The letter of James says, according to the Authorized Version, 'Ye have heard of the patience of Job' (James 5:11). There is no more impatient book in the Old Testament than the book of Job! It is one long protest against seeming injustice. But the Revised English Bible has it, 'You have heard *how Job stood firm*, and you have seen how the Lord treated him in the end, for the Lord is merciful and compassionate'. That is the correct translation of James 5:11.

'Patience', or endurance, is one of the marks of the Spirit-filled life (Galatians 5:22). By its exercise, the Christian grows muscle. It is an important ingredient in the list of things which Paul speaks of in Romans 5:3–4. Jesus displayed it—'he endured the cross, ignoring its disgrace…' (Hebrews 12:2).

Psalm 13 begins with protest (vv. 1 and 2), 'How long, Lord?'; goes on to prayer (vv. 3–4), 'Look now, Lord my God, and answer me'; ends with praise (vv. 5, 6), 'I shall sing to the Lord, for he has granted all my desire.' It is a good progression. Possibly a pattern for our prayer-life?

PRAYER

Direct my heart, O God, towards the steadfastness of Christ.

Note: comment on Psalm 14 will be found on pages 124 and 125, with Psalm 53.

The PRESENCE *of the* HOLY ONE

As we read this short psalm we can envisage a group of people from the villages of the Holy Land going up to Jerusalem for one of the great feasts. It was an awe-inspiring experience—who should be allowed to visit the great temple and share in its worship? As the group nears the building, they meet one of the priests and ask him the question on their minds. The answer comes with a clarity which is searching: let them examine themselves by the tests mentioned in verses 2–5. They are strictly ethical. The examination must reach heart (v. 2), tongue, relationship with neighbours (v. 3), finances, and general uprightness of character (v. 5). Interestingly, the emphasis on the tongue reminds us of Psalm 12. Only when this examination has taken place should they engage in the worship of Israel's God (v. 1).

We can note that God's 'tent' (v. 1) was the portable sanctuary where God met with his people during the long years of their wandering in the wilderness. Divided into three parts (the vestibule, the holy place, and the holy of holies), it could be dismantled and re-assembled as the people moved on. The use of the word 'tent' is a reminder of those days of wandering. God's 'holy mountain' (v. 1) was Zion, where, in great magnificence, the temple was later built as a permanent meeting place with God.

The priest's answer to the would-be worshippers enshrines a time-less warning—we should not rush, unprepared, into the presence of the Holy One. Beware of over-familiarity with God. Beware a lack of awe.

Participating in the feast

When Paul was writing to the Corinthians, he found he had to issue a warning about their eucharistic gatherings. There were indications that, when they broke the bread and took the cup and so proclaimed the Lord's death until he comes, they did so unworthily and thus were 'guilty of offending against the body and blood of the Lord. Everyone must test himself before eating from the bread or drinking from the cup' (1 Corinthians 11:23–32). We need to heed the warning, especially in days when the very frequency of celebration of the Holy Communion can—and in some cases does—lead to a casual approach to the mystery and the awesome privilege of participation in the feast.

The list in verses 2–5 is a searching one. It is basic to the creation and maintenance of a healthy society. Those who follow these lines of conduct will not only themselves 'remain unshaken' (v. 5), but will also provide a stable element without which society will collapse into chaos. A strong input of such people in the business world, the legal world, the homes of the people, will serve as an antiseptic element in society. Jesus spoke of such people—'you are salt *to the world*'. The world is dark and the forces of darkness are powerful—'you are light *for all the world*' (Matthew 5:13–14).

We should do well to stop at this point and read Psalm 15 and Matthew 5:13–16 together. Then we could turn our reading and thinking into a prayer provided by another psalm:

PRAYER

Examine me, God, and know my mind;
test me, and understand my anxious thoughts.
Watch lest I follow any path that grieves you;
lead me in the everlasting way.

Psalm 139:23–24

The VOICE *of the* FORTUNATE

This is the psalm of a happy man. I think I can see him: he is happy with his position in life—the lines have fallen to him in pleasant places and he is well content (v. 6). And not only in material things is he fortunate—he knows where to find wisdom, and he blesses God for that (v. 7). Clearly, he is a godly man. He is on talking terms with God, calling him *my* Lord (v. 2), and tells us what he said when he prayed (vv. 2–6). He conceives God as being very close, at his 'right hand' (v. 8).

He would appear to have been a leader in his community (or perhaps his nation). He is at pains to surround himself with godly men who were worshippers of the one true God (vv. 3, 4), rather as a Christian Prime Minister might choose men and women of similar conviction to himself to strengthen his cabinet.

When he refers to the Lord as being his 'cup' (v. 5), an unusual description, he may well be thinking of him as the source of his refreshment, as a drink is to a hot and thirsty person and as the source of his delight, as a glass of wine turns a drab meal into a feast.

Future joy

This God whom he holds in honour in his daily affairs will not allow him, when this life is over, to go down to Sheol, the pit, the place of darkness. However dim may be the psalmist's concept of the future life, there would seem to be in verse 11 some measure of assurance of future joy: 'You will show me the path of life; in your presence is the fulness of joy, at your right hand are pleasures for evermore.'

In Peter's address at Pentecost to his fellow Jews, he quoted—with considerable freedom—from verses 7–11 and referred them to the resurrection of Jesus by the power of God (Acts 2:25ff.). In similar fashion, Paul at Antioch used verse 10 as one of a little series of 'proof texts' from the Old Testament about Jesus who did not 'suffer corruption' but was raised to new life by God's activity (Acts 13:35).

These verses take on a richer and fuller meaning when they are seen through the eyes of a Christian rejoicing in the resurrection of Jesus Christ. The believer's 'heart is glad' (v. 9), his hope is sure (v. 10), and his anticipation of life in the presence of God himself (v. 11) is keen.

We can be grateful to this happy psalmist for admitting us to the secrets of his confidence and joy.

REFLECTION

My aim: To 'set the Lord before me at all times' (v. 8).

My prayer: 'Keep me, God, for in you I have found refuge' (v. 1).

My praise: 'I shall bless the Lord who has given me counsel' (v. 7).

15   PSALM 17

NOT BOASTING, *but* GROANING

On first reading, this might seem to be the prayer of a man well satisfied with his spiritual state, even proud of it. His lips are 'innocent of all deceit' (v. 1); there is 'no malice in him' (v. 3); his steps have 'held steadily' to God's paths (v. 5); his 'plea is just' (v. 15). Maybe. But there is another way of looking at this man. He is grappling with a problem: why do the wicked get away with it, while the righteous suffer? Is this psalm more of a groan than a boast?

If it is, Bishop Lancelot Andrewes (1555–1626) in his *Private Prayers* may help us. He wrote: 'More is done by groanings than by words: to this end Christ groaned, for to give us an ensample of groaning. It is not that God desireth us to be suppliant or loveth that we lie prostrate: the profit thereof is ours and it hath regard to our advantage'.

No complete answer

Have we not, all of us, sometimes cried out in our praying: 'Life is unfair. Why does God allow his children, who seek to follow him, to suffer, while those who do not give a thought to him appear to prosper?' There is no easy answer. There will be no complete answer this side of heaven. Paul knew that—we can watch him wrestle with it in Romans 8, and we note particularly verse 23, 'we also, to whom the Spirit is given as the firstfruits of the harvest to come, are groaning inwardly while we look forward eagerly to our adoption, our liberation from mortality'—and verse 26, 'In the same way the Spirit comes to the aid of our weakness. We do not even know how we ought to pray, but through our inarticulate groans the Spirit himself is pleading for us.' He gives no easy answer, but he sheds much light on the problem. His wrestling, his groaning, became a blessing to him and to generations of those who have pondered his words.

Praying for enemies

The psalmist's enemies are sketched in vivid colours—they are violent (v. 9), compassionless, proud (v. 10), lion-like, hungry for their prey (v. 12), and so on. What does he pray for them? That God will 'make an end of them' and 'thrust them out of this world from among the living' (vv. 13, 14). Perhaps the uttering of such a pitiless prayer brought the psalmist a measure of relief. We can only contrast it with the teaching which Jesus was to give, some centuries later, and which still stands as a challenge and often as a rebuke to his followers: 'You have heard that they were told, "Love your neighbour and hate your enemy". But what I tell you is this: Love your enemies and pray for your persecutors; only so can you be children of your heavenly Father...' (Matthew 5:43–45).

Through all the wrestling and against the background of his suffering, our psalmist knows that God's unfailing love is marvellous (v. 7), and he dares to pray the prayer (v. 8) which for long centuries has been prayed by the church in the service of Compline:

PRAYER

Guard me like the apple of your eye;
hide me in the shadow of your wings.

The LANGUAGE of LOVE

'I love you, Lord.' This is a long psalm. We should do well to stop at the end of its opening four words, and to go no further till we have looked them in the eye. 'I love you, Lord'. It is an astonishing statement: this tiny human being looks into the face of Almighty God and says from a full heart, 'I love you.' Few devotees of other religions than Judaism and Christianity would dare to say this.

What does it mean when Christians take these words on their lips? We shall best understand this by considering the analogy of the love of a man for a woman, for this itself is a gift from God, the great Lover. What does he mean when he says to her, 'I love you'? He acknowledges:

- his *gratitude* to her. In responding to his love, she has revealed the miracle, perhaps not hitherto fully recognized by him, that he is a lovable human being. He has a new conception of his worthwhileness from this point on.

- his *admiration*. He admires her physical attractiveness and rejoices in it. But he also recognizes the quality of her character. In his estimation, she is a great human being. 'Admire' is from the Latin word to *wonder*—to regard with pleased surprise. Wonder is next door to worship. So:

- his *reverence* for her—his respect, his deference, his courteous regard, his worship (in the sense that that word is used in the 1662 Marriage Service—'with my body I thee worship').

- his *willingness to commit himself* to her and to live in the light of that gratitude, admiration and reverence which he feels for her. That commitment must, in the nature of the case, be for life.

These are four of the elements that go to the make-up of human love, and, even more certainly, of a person's love for God. They are constituents in our response to the first of the two commandments that Jesus quoted (Mark 12:30; Deuteronomy 6:5). 'You must love the Lord your God with all your heart... soul... mind... strength.' Perhaps the greatest of the four elements is gratitude. When I look at the cross I say: 'If that is the measure of the love of God for me, I'm *grateful*.'

Transcendence and immanence

The language in which God is described (vv. 7–15) is terrifying. This God, smoke proceeding from his nostrils, fire from his mouth, parting the heavens, swooping on the wings of the wind, thundering from the heavens, hurling forth lightning shafts, exposing earth's foundations, *this God* 'reached down from on high and took me, drew me... delivered me... rescued me because he delighted in me' (vv. 16–19). How could human language describe God's transcendence (his greatness) and his immanence (his nearness) better than this? *He* took *me*.

Augustine writes about 'eternal life promised to us through the humility of our God, coming down to our pride' (*Confessions*). He was thinking of the incarnation, of him who 'was rich yet for our sakes became poor'. We cannot do anything for our self-redemption. We can only be rescued 'from above'.

> *Something has to happen that I myself cannot cause to happen. I cannot be reborn from below; that is, with my own strength, with my own mind, with my own psychological insights. There is no doubt in my mind about this because I have tried so hard in the past to heal myself from my complaints and failed... and failed... and failed, until I came to the edge of complete emotional collapse and even physical exhaustion. I can only be healed from above, from where God reaches down. What is impossible for me is possible for God.* (Henri Nouwen, *The Return of the Prodigal Son*)

I must be 'born from above' (John 3:3, literal translation).

REFLECTION

I sought the Lord, and afterward I knew
He moved my soul to seek him, seeking me;
It was not I that found, O Saviour true;
No, I was found of thee.
Thou didst reach forth thy hand and mine enfold;
I walked and sank not on the storm-vexed sea;
'Twas not so much that I on thee took hold
As thou, dear Lord, on me.
I find, I walk, I love, but oh, the whole
Of love is but my answer, Lord, to thee!
For thou wast long beforehand with my soul;
Always thou lovedst me.

17 PSALM 19

CHAOS & ORDER

I confess to a feeling of oppression, not to say of terror, when I consider the picture of the universe which scientists such as Fred Hoyle and Stephen Hawking give us. It is a picture of space so vast as to be incomprehensible to our mind; of worlds of exploding gases and unimaginable heat and cold. Our little world is a mere dot in space, and we mortals…? I shiver.

Not so our psalmist. He had no idea of the immensity of the universe which the scientists have discovered, nor, for that matter, of the size of the earth on which he lived. But two things struck him—he would say *spoke* to him: the regularity of the world's order (day after day, night after night, season after season), and the power of the sun. This ordered rhythm, this life-giving heat spoke to him though no words were necessary. They were a sign; they had a message (v. 4). They spoke to him of the glory of God (v. 1). The God who spoke and chaos gave place to order, the God who spoke and darkness became light (Genesis 1), was *his* God. No wonder that Haydn's choral work 'The heavens are telling…' is full of verve and excitement.

Paul, in a passage which has no parallel in his other writings, touches on this matter in Romans 1:20: 'Ever since the world began [God's] invisible attributes, that is to say his everlasting power and deity, have been visible to the eye of reason, in the things he has made.' The argument is elaborated further in Wisdom 13:1–9.

Psalmist and apostle had ears to hear. We would do well to sharpen our hearing apparatus.

Four-fold pattern

This remarkable psalm is divided into four parts, the first two parts, different from one another as they first appear, being closely connected:

- God's revelation in creation (vv. 1–6). We need open eyes.
- God's revelation through the law (vv. 7–11). We need obedient feet to walk in God's paths.

56

- A glimpse of the psalmist's own religion (vv. 12, 13). We need deliverance from evil.

- A prayer (v. 14). We need guarded tongues.

The law of the Lord

In verses 7–11 the writer switches from nature to law, but only to expound them *both* as media through which God deals with and speaks to his people. What is meant by 'the *law* of the Lord'? It is a word which constantly recurs in the psalms and is elaborated at great length in Psalm 119. It is sometimes used in just the same sense as we use the word in English, for example in Exodus 12:49, 'The same law will apply both to the native-born and to the alien...' But it is very frequently used in a wider sense, for example the law given through Moses; and then, even more widely, in the sense of teaching, instruction coming from God, through human agency, for the welfare of those who will receive it and live by it. It is in this last sense that the word is used in verses 7–11: teaching which comes from the Lord, instruction, guidance, divine revelation.

In these verses, the general word 'law' is broken down by mention of some of its constituent parts—instruction (v. 7), precepts, commandments (v. 8), judgments (v. 9). This teaching, so far from cramping its hearers, 'revives the soul' (v. 7), gives 'joy to the heart', 'light to the eyes' (v. 8), warning in danger (v. 11). It makes for an integrated personality. It marks a happy man (see Psalm 1). 'In obeying them there is great reward' (v. 11).

REFLECTION

I have rejoiced in the path of your instruction
as one rejoices over wealth of every kind...
In your statutes I find continual delight;
I shall not forget your word.

Psalm 119:14, 16

18   PSALM 19

Living Under *the* Eyes *of* God

Through nature then (vv. 1–6) and through God's instruction (vv. 7–11), God deals graciously with his people. From that wide background, the psalmist now turns to a brief reference to his own life lived under the eye of God:

> *Who is aware of his unwitting sins?*
> *Cleanse me of any secret fault.*
> *Hold back your servant also from wilful sins,*
> *lest they get the better of me.*
> *Then I shall be blameless,*
> *innocent of grave offence'* (vv. 12, 13).

He is conscious of his own frailty and tendency to sin.

Two categories of sin

He mentions two categories of sin—the unwitting sins, and the wilful sins. '*Unwitting*'—is it possible to sin in this way? I take it to mean sins due to ignorance, sins which he did not recognize as sins because his conscience was too ill-educated to discern right from wrong. There is such a thing as culpable ignorance—when we have not worked at the implications of being men or women of God.

And '*wilful* sins'—we know about them all too well! We have experience of habits which have dragged on and dragged us down and have led us to sin. If we fail to turn our backs on them, our conscience becomes insensitive, and the voice of the God of love who would lead us in his paths becomes less clear.

More listening

So our writer turns to prayer (v. 14)—a prayer about *mouth* and *mind* (v. 14). Churchgoers will recognize it as a prayer often used by preachers before the sermon. It could hardly be bettered for such occasions. But it asks for a much wider use than that. It is a fine prayer with which to begin each day. How many words will pass my lips today? How many thoughts will occupy my mind? Too many words, probably—we talk too much, too many trivialities, too much nonsense, too many unkindnesses. *Mindless* talk? Note how the psalmist joins words of mouth with thoughts of mind. The mouth is the outlet of the mind and heart. Our aim, then, should be: less talking, less gossip; more listening, more openness to others' needs. Our passion should be to be 'acceptable' to God.

PRAYER

May the words of my mouth
and the thoughts of my mind
be acceptable to you,
Lord, my rock and my redeemer! (v. 14)

19

STRENGTH *in* TIMES *of* TROUBLE

It often happens that a particular piece of literature is associated in our mind with some particular event in our experience. I can rarely hear Psalm 20, read or sung, without its recalling to me an event which took place in 1946. I was in Lincoln Cathedral attending Bishop Leslie Owen at his enthronement. Shortly before the end of the Second World War, he had been in the Guards' Chapel in London when it was hit by one of Hitler's flying bombs. Because he was standing behind a pillar, the bishop survived. At his enthronement, we sang this psalm. I noticed that the bishop's hand was shaking as he held his service paper. Why? It may well have been the thought of the huge responsibility which would be his as bishop of that great diocese. It may have been that the results of that bombing were already taking effect in his body—he died in 1947. But he knew where to find his strength in time of need—'may the Lord answer you in time of trouble... send you help from the sanctuary... give you support from Zion' (vv. 1, 2).

On the way to battle

This is one of the so-called royal psalms which we find scattered throughout the Psalter. One might be used at a coronation or anniversary such as Psalms 2 or 72, another at a royal wedding (Psalm 45); another before going into battle. Psalm 20 belongs to the last category.

The king is embarking on a military exercise. The religious leader prays for strength and support from God (vv. 1, 2), and for a successful outcome from the battle: 'May he give you your heart's desire, and grant success to all your plans' (v. 4). In confident anticipation, he bids the congregation sing aloud in praise of the king's victory, while doing homage to the God who answers prayer (v. 5).

'His anointed one' (v. 6) is, of course, the king himself—kings as well as priests were anointed on taking office. The psalmist sees the victory as already won—'the Lord *has* given victory to his anointed one' (v. 6), though the successful answer to the people's prayer is yet future—we note the verb tenses in verse 6. The source of their confidence is God himself (v. 7). The enemy will 'totter and fall'; the king and his supporters will 'rise up and stand firm' (v. 8). The psalm ends with a prayer for the king.

The king in ancient times was himself the centre of power in a way that no monarch can be in modern times. In our day the power is shared, and the Queen is a *symbol* of governmental power. Executive power rests in the hands of Prime Minister, Cabinet, Houses of Parliament, the voting men and women. Worldwide there are now few monarchies in existence. On those of us who have a royal house it is incumbent to *pray*—'Lord, save the Queen'. More prayer—less criticism; that is the way to a truly successful government.

PRAYER

For those in power we pray:
On them may the spirit of the Lord rest,
a spirit of wisdom and understanding,
a spirit of counsel and power,
a spirit of knowledge and fear of the Lord.

Isaiah 11:2

VICTORY PRAISE

Psalm 21 seems to follow logically on Psalm 20. The king has been to battle and has won an outstanding victory. God has blessed him.

The psalm falls into two parts with an ascription of praise at the end (v. 13). The first part is addressed to God (vv. 1–7); the second part is addressed to the king (vv. 8–12).

Verses 1–7 tell us who the greatest actor in the drama of war has been—not the troops, not even the king who led them into battle. It has been God himself. The king is subject to no man, but he is subject to God. Addressing God, the psalmist (perhaps the leader of the people's worship) ascribes the glory to God alone: 'You have granted him his heart's desire' (v. 2); 'you welcome him with blessings...' (v. 3); 'you gave him' life (v. 4); 'you invest him with majesty and honour' (v. 5), and so on. There is no room for pride or boasting here. The subject-king owes all to God. Let him remember that. No *hubris!*—no overwhelming pride.

The prophets constantly inveighed against human wrongness which expressed itself in the sin of pride. For them, Babylon stood as the supreme example of national pride. But pride comes before a fall, and in Isaiah chapter 14, the prophet uttered a taunt-song against the king of Babylon to illustrate this point. It is a brilliant piece of writing: 'bright morning star, how you have fallen from heaven... !' (Isaiah 14:12).

In Luke 10:17ff. Jesus welcomed back the seventy-two after their evangelistic mission. He rejoiced with them that the powers of darkness had been defeated by the disciples' word. 'I saw Satan fall, like lightning, from heaven...' (v. 18). The power of God had been at work not by the preaching of the 'learned and wise' but by the witness of the 'simple', the people who were divested of their pride and clothed in the power of God. No room for boasting here. Again, no *hubris!*

Living through conflict

In verses 8–12, the psalmist turns to address the king. The language reminds those of us who lived through World War II all too vividly of the conquerors' talk in the latter stages and at the conclusion of the conflict—'destroy their offspring… rid mankind of their posterity…' (v. 10); 'to hell with Germans and Japs and all their brood'. War breeds hate; the flames of vengeance burn high. Paul, I know, was thinking in *personal* rather than international terms when he wrote to the Romans: 'My dear friends, do not seek revenge, but leave a place for divine retribution; for there is a text which reads, "Vengeance is mine, says the Lord, I will repay"' (Romans 12:19). But nations as well as individuals do well to bear his injunction in mind.

The psalm ends with an ascription of glory to God (v. 13). Honour where honour is due! 'We shall sing a psalm of praise to your power.'

LET US PRAISE

All glory, laud, and honour
to thee, Redeemer, King.

John Mason Neale (1818–60)

To God the Father, God the Son, and God the Holy Spirit,
be ascribed, as are most justly due,
all might, majesty, dominion, and power
now and for ever.

CRYING AGAINST GOD

Jesus knew his scriptures (what we call the Old Testament). Probably his mother taught him about them, and quoted them to him when he was a boy. Certainly he heard them read and expounded when, Saturday by Saturday, he went, with other members of the family, to the local synagogue. His spiritual life was strengthened by his meditation on these scriptures, including the psalms. In the long and dreadful hours on the cross, he reverted to them; two of the seven words from the cross are quotations from the psalms—the last cry 'Father, into your hands I commit my spirit' (Luke 23:46) is from Psalm 31:5. The other is the opening of Psalm 22—'my God, my God, why have you forsaken me?' (Matthew 27:46). A well-stored mind can be of help in times of dire distress. We shall return to Jesus' quotation of this verse a little later. But first, a look at the psalm as a whole.

Its colours are dark, its imagery vivid. The opening verses are a protest, an accusation against God. In the old days, God had obviously listened when Israel's ancient leaders had cried to him (vv. 2–5), but now the writer is being mocked by his enemies precisely because he is so obviously abandoned by God (vv. 6–8)! Right from birth he had been entrusted to God (vv. 9, 10). But now in his darkest hour, God is far off and he himself has no helper (v. 11).

Exactly what form his trouble took is not clear. There was certainly a physical element to it—he is weak, his 'mouth is dry' (vv. 14, 15), 'this poor body' (v. 21) is in deep distress. As for his enemies, he compares them to a herd of 'great bulls' (v. 12), 'ravening lions' (v. 13), 'hounds and ruffians' (v. 16)—no more need be said! But what is worst of all is his sense of dereliction by God (vv. 1, 2, 19). And it was *this* that wrung the cry from Jesus on the cross.

Obedience through suffering

Jesus was carrying a load the like of which none of us will ever be called upon to bear. 'He carried our sins in his own person on the gibbet', as Peter put it in his first letter (1 Peter 2:24). It was a crushing load which blotted out for Jesus the consciousness of the presence of the God who had meant more to him, all his life, than anyone or anything else. If the cross is the place where God's disgust with sin and his burning love for humankind meet in terrible expression; if God in Christ is there clearing up the mess made by a rebel race, can we wonder that there is mystery? We can dare to look—and adore.

Jesus did not conceal the question that tortured him. He did not repress it nor attempt to swallow it. He gave expression to it as other psalmists had done—'why stand far off, Lord? Why hide away in times of trouble?' (Psalm 10:1). Why? 'Why have you forsaken me?' In this cry, we are faced, as perhaps nowhere else, with the reality of the human nature of Jesus, and in this I find comfort—as did the writer of the letter to the Hebrews: 'In the course of his earthly life [Jesus] offered up prayers and petitions, with loud cries and tears, to God who was able to deliver him from death. Because of his devotion his prayer was heard: son though he was, *he learned obedience through his sufferings*' (Hebrews 5:7–8).

Transformation

There is another point of importance to note about this psalm. From verse 22 the whole tone is different from the verses which precede it. The key turns from minor to major: 'I shall declare your fame to my associates, praising you'.

To every sensitive person come moments when a sense of dereliction threatens to overwhelm them. What is the meaning of human history? Why the immensity of human suffering? Is Christianity a piece of make-believe? The death of a dear one, the sickness of another—is there not one clear word from beyond? Belief is easy when spring is in the air and everyone smiles on you. There are winter moments when all is dark. 'My God, my God, why... ?'

Those of us who are in darkness, whether it is the darkness of doubt or of bereavement or of any other kind, can take heart. The sun is still there, though the clouds now are hiding it. The Father is still there, though his face seems to be hidden. Christ knows and understands, because he has been through experiences worse even than those you are now enduring. The darkness is not for ever.

MEDITATION

Did you ever watch on television or in a garden an expert pruning a vine? I did, and I thought it seemed so cruel: the thrust of the pruning-knife went so close to the roots. But I noticed that the gardener was never nearer the vine than when he was pruning it.

PASTORAL SCENES

Of all the psalms this is the best known and best loved. It is solace to the bereaved on the occasion of funerals and memorial services. Its popularity is in large part due to the tune 'Crimond' to which it is frequently sung. It conjures up sylvan pictures of the countryside, running brooks, fattening sheep—a soothing scene.

Few of those who join in the psalm on such occasions realize how tough and, often, dangerous were the life and work of a shepherd in biblical times. Young shepherd David said to King Saul: 'Whenever a lion or a bear comes and carries off a sheep… I go after it and attack it… and batter it to death…' (1 Samuel 17:34, 35). The rescue of a lamb fallen over a precipice was risky work. There were dark valleys where marauders hid. Psalm 23 depicts the scene as the writer would *like* things to be—green pastures and plenty of water (v. 2), clear paths (v. 3), plenty of food and drink (v. 5) and, work done, a secure home: 'Goodness and love unfailing will follow me all the days of my life' (v. 6).

Spiritually what did this all mean to the writer of the psalm, and what should its metaphors mean to us three thousand years later—the numbers of us who live in great conurbations and to whom all the rustic vocabulary seems foreign?

A generous and tender God

If we look at it with fresh eyes, we see that the writer is primarily concerned with *God*—note the recurrence of *he* (vv. 1–4a), and, in as much as the psalm is a meditation or prayer, *you* (vv. 4b–5)—God the carer, God the reviver, God the rescuer and comforter, God the lavish host. It is this affirmation of a generous and tender God which gives him courage and assurance as he faces the future (v. 6).

The Bible is full of shepherd imagery. I would suggest that it would be well, before passing on to another psalm, to stop and read carefully two passages which take up the shepherd–sheep picture, Ezekiel 34 and John 10. Ezekiel 34 begins with a denunciation of false shepherds (vv. 1–10): 'The Lord God says: I am against the shepherds and shall demand from them an account of my sheep. I shall dismiss those shepherds from tending my flock: no longer will they care only for themselves; I shall rescue my sheep from their mouths, and they will feed on them no more' (v. 10) and goes on to elaborate God's own shepherding work in rescuing and providing for the flock (vv. 11–16). John 10:1–18 is the well-known picture of Jesus as the good shepherd, prepared to lay down his life in defence of his sheep—the accent again on the rescue work involved and on the shepherd's determination to see that the flock has life 'in all its fulness'. 'I am the good shepherd; I know my own and my own know me, as the Father knows me and I know the Father; and I lay down my life for the sheep' (John 10:14–15). It is a costly business, but Jesus loved 'to the uttermost' (see John 13:1)—and still does.

PRAYER

My dearest Lord,
Be thou a bright flame before me,
Be thou a guiding star above me,
Be thou a smooth path beneath me,
Be thou a kindly shepherd before me,
Today and evermore.

Columba

GOD'S CARETAKERS

'To the Lord belong the earth and everything in it' (v. 1). But humans are entrusted with it; they are its caretakers on behalf of the Creator. The responsibility is vast. Of what character should these caretakers be? The answer is sketched in verses 3–6. It is given in terms that are starkly ethical, moral rather than ritual, reminding us of the similar thoughts expressed in Psalm 15.

They 'go up the mountain of the Lord', they 'stand in his holy place' (v. 3), that is to say, they are *worshippers*. No mention is made of what they bring (usually tithes or sacrificial offerings); the accent is wholly on what they are—their hands are clean, their hearts pure (v. 4). We are reminded of the teaching of Jesus in Matthew 5:23–24, about a man going to the altar and recollecting that he is in a bad relationship with his brother. What is he to do? Drop his gift and make his peace with his brother. Only then can he expect his gift to be accepted. We note the prophet's insistence on God's disgust with worship offered by people with blood on their hands—the reek of their sacrifices is abhorrent to him. (See, for example, Isaiah 1:10–17 and Amos 5:21ff.) Morals matter more than ritual.

With our knowledge of cosmology, the idea of a world 'founded on the seas' and 'planted on the waters beneath' (v. 2) is strange to us. It reflects the idea of a myth prevalent in the Ancient Near East which depicts God as victor over chaos, defeating the monster of destruction and death (see Psalm 74:12ff.). The language reminds us of the first of the two creation stories in the opening two chapters of Genesis. The sea spoke to the Israelites of all that was threatening to human stability. The wicked themselves 'are like a storm-tossed sea, a sea that cannot be still, whose waters cast up mud and dirt' (Isaiah 57:20).

At the temple gates

The rest of the psalm, verses 7–10, gives a vivid sketch of a procession of worshippers going up to seek the presence of God at the temple on Jerusalem's hill. Its members are carrying the most sacred symbol of their worship, the Ark (dealt with further in my comments on Psalm 47). The great gates are shut. The worshippers cry: 'Lift up your heads, you gates... that the King of glory may come in' (v. 7). A voice inside the temple shouts: 'Who is this King of glory?' Back comes the reply: 'The Lord strong and mighty, the Lord mighty in battle'. With full dramatic effect, the question and answer are repeated (vv. 9, 10). We can almost see the gate swing open and the crowds pressing in—to offer their worship to the Lord of all the earth (v. 1), the God of Jacob (v. 6), the King of glory, the Lord strong and mighty, the Lord mighty in battle (vv. 8, 10).

Let us WORSHIP

Most High, omnipotent, good Lord,
To you be ceaseless praise outpoured
And blessing without measure.
Let every creature thankful be
And serve in great humility.

Based on a prayer of Francis of Assisi (*Celebrating Common Prayer*)

A Pupil *of* Prayer

We may well be grateful for this psalm. It is intensely personal. We are allowed to overhear a man of God at his prayers, and that is a privilege. He has much that will help us if we take our prayer life seriously.

Clearly, the psalmist sees himself as a pupil, a learner, a disciple. 'Teach me your ways' (v. 4); 'lead me' and 'teach me' (v. 5), he prays. And he sees God as the great teacher—'he teaches sinners… he guides the humble… and teaches them his way' (vv. 8, 9). It is a lovely relationship and, once established, never grows stale, so that, when we are old, we know that we are only at the beginning of the road of discovery. 'The Holy Spirit… will teach you everything,' Jesus is recorded as saying, 'and remind you of all that I have told you' (John 14:26).

Guided by God

The subject of divine guidance is not an easy one. But our psalmist has some light to shed on it. 'Whoever *fears* the Lord will be shown the path…' (v. 12). 'The Lord confides his purposes to those who *fear* him' (v. 14). What does he mean by 'fear'? Certainly there is no idea here of being scared of God—'in love there is no room for fear; indeed, perfect love banishes fear' (1 John 4:18). To fear God is so to reverence him that we seek to align our will with his; to avoid anything which would grieve him. An attitude like this leads into such a relationship with God that he lets us into his secrets, 'confides his purposes to' us (v. 14). 'We possess the mind of Christ,' Paul dared to say (1 Corinthians 2:16).

Arrow prayers

I can see this psalmist as a man who was accustomed to using *arrow prayers*, those quick looks Godwards during the busyness of a day in the midst of activity. He is perplexed. 'Teach me *your* ways,' he prays (v. 4). He is at a crossroads. 'Lead me… and teach me,' he prays (v. 5). He has slipped and sinned. 'Forgive my wickedness,' he prays (v. 16). He is scared stiff. 'Defend me and deliver me,' he prays (v. 20). So he keeps in touch, through the hours of the day, with a God who listens to the cry of his servant.

There are depths of prayer on which our psalmist does not touch. But the use of arrow prayers is a good beginning and, if adopted, might well become a lifetime habit. That is much to be desired.

A *personal* psalm. Yes, but before it closes, the psalmist looks to God for the nation he loves. 'God, deliver Israel from all their troubles' (v. 22)—the things that degrade a nation—materialism, sleaze, class distinction, the sheer stupidity of godlessness. From such things, good Lord, deliver us.

PRAYER

Lead me, Lord, lead me in your righteousness.
Make your way plain before my face.

Happy is the nation whose God is the Lord.

Psalm 33:12

25

A PRIESTLY PSALMIST

It sounds as if the writer of this psalm was a priest. He washes his hands 'to go in procession round your altar, Lord, recounting your marvellous deeds, making them known with thankful hearts' (vv. 6, 7). There is an interesting passage in Exodus where God instructs Moses to make a bronze basin for ablution. In it Aaron and his sons are to wash their hands and feet when they enter the Tent of Meeting and when they approach the altar to minister. This was a statute binding on Aaron and his descendants (Exodus 30:17–21). Similarly, Isaiah charges his priestly leaders: 'Keep yourselves pure, you that carry the vessels of the Lord' (Isaiah 52:11). This priestly psalmist loves the temple where he is called to minister, the house where God dwells and his glory resides (v. 8), the 'full assembly' where he blesses God (v. 12).

If this is the case, it goes far to explain the language in which the writer protests his innocence and his purity of life. On first reading, we resent the language of such verses as 1, 4, 5, 11: 'Lord, uphold my cause, for I have led a blameless life, and put unfailing trust in you' (v. 1); 'I have not sat among the worthless, nor do I associate with hypocrites' (v. 4); 'I detest the company of evildoers, nor shall I sit among the ungodly' (v. 5); 'But I lead a blameless life; deliver me and show your favour' (v. 11). The man seems self-righteous, superior, boastful. We have heard that those who know God best are the most aware of their own sinfulness. That is the ground of their humility. Not so this writer. He appears cocksure of his own righteousness.

Deep spirituality

But is this really so? I doubt it. I see here a man who is so conscious of the privilege of being called to be a priest of God, to go in procession round the altar, to recount God's marvellous deeds to the assembled people, that he is simply stating the fact that he has watched his step as to the company he keeps and the circumstances which might lead him to soil his hands and lose his soul.

There are hints of a deep spirituality. He lives by the faithfulness of God: 'for your constant love is before my eyes' (v. 3). God's faithfulness to him, God's utter reliability, is the undergirding strength of his life. God will never let him out of his grasp. The confident 'I lead a blameless life' is balanced by the humble prayer, 'deliver me and show me your favour' (v. 11).

Those who are spiritual leaders in our generation have no easy task. They are often the butt of a secular press and the objects of criticism thrown at them by their own people. The Church would be the stronger if its members, for every criticism they offer, would pray for them instead. To help us in our prayers we might use the words of the prayer for the Ordination of Priests in the *Alternative Service Book 1980*:

PRAYER

Give them wisdom and discipline to work faithfully with all their fellow-servants in Christ, that the world may come to know your glory and your love. Accept our prayers, most merciful Father, through your Son Jesus Christ our Lord...

GOD *is* WITH US

The French have a word for it—*insouciance*. It means carefreeness, unconcernedness, light-heartedness. That is the predominant note of this psalm. The writer is certainly a realist. He is not fool enough to suggest that because a person is godly, all his problems are solved. Not at all: there are adversaries, enemies (v. 2); there are days of darkness and misfortune (v. 5). But the psalm rings with the overpowering conviction of the presence of the Lord, of the assurance that he may be sought and found in his temple (v. 4), his tent (v. 5). Even though—he posits the most unlikely situation—even though his father and mother were to forsake him (v. 10) there would be One to take him into his care, the Lord himself. With verse 10 we may compare Isaiah 49:15—'Can a woman forget the infant at her breast, or a mother the child of her womb? But should even these forget, I shall never forget you.'

The little soliloquy of verse 8 passes into a plea that God will not reject or forsake the writer, but there is an underlying conviction that that will never happen. Such a possibility is denied in the opening verse with its note of defiance—'whom should I fear... of whom should I go in dread?' It reminds us of the defiant questions and answers which Paul throws at his readers in his letter to the Romans: 'Who will bring a charge... ? Not God... Who will pronounce judgment? Not Christ... What can separate us from the love of Christ...? I am convinced that there is nothing in death or life... nothing in all creation that can separate us from the love of God in Christ Jesus our Lord' (Romans 8:31–39).

That is the ground of the psalmist's *insouciance*.

Learning the way of the Lord

This confidence, however, does not come to us at the drop of a hat. It is deepened as the psalmist gazes on the beauty of the Lord, seeks him in his temple (v. 4) and is prepared to be taught the way of the Lord (v. 11). Steady learning of the Lord's way, the principles on which he works, the grace he longs to bestow, the resources he has at his disposal—these things come to those who are prepared to 'wait for the Lord'. *They* become brave and strong. They have grounds for hope (v. 14).

It is out of a deep experience of God's faithfulness and availability that the psalmist turns from addressing God (vv. 1–13) to challenge his audience, whoever and wherever they may be (v. 14). 'Wait for the Lord,' he says; 'be strong and brave, and put your hope in the Lord.'

To **PONDER**

Today might well provide an opportunity to put verse 14 into action; or to share it with someone in need of the confidence which marks this psalm as a whole. 'Wait for the Lord, be strong and brave, and put your hope in the Lord.'

Alone with none but thee, my God,
I journey on my way.
What need I fear, when thou art near,
O King of night and day?
More safe I am within thy hand
Than if a host did round me stand.

Columba

27

SHELTERED *by the* ROCK

'My Rock' (v. 1). 'Dear Lord', we often say when beginning a prayer. I do not think I have ever heard a prayer which began 'Dear Rock'! But it would have been in harmony with the way in which the psalmists thought of God. They refer to God in this way at least sixteen times.

We say of a good friend, 'She's rocklike.' We mean that we could turn to her at any time and find her steady. She is dependable, trustworthy, unchanging.

The writer of this psalm was presumably very familiar with the story of the long years in which his people had wandered en route to the promised land. Sometimes, when a storm blew up or a band of marauders was ready to pounce, it was a matter of life and death to find a rocky shelter—for shepherds and sheep alike. Now, in this psalm, he sees his people menaced by 'the ungodly—evildoers—with malice in their hearts' (v. 3). They need a shelter from this storm of iniquity. The psalmist knows where this is to be found—in God, the Rock, the steady and unchanging one.

He may well have recalled the incident when the Israelites were parched with thirst, and Moses struck the rock and the waters poured out (Exodus 17:1–7). Again the psalmist knows where refreshment and renewal are to be found—in God, his Rock. To him he calls 'with hands uplifted towards your holy shrine' (v. 2).

In verses 4 and 5 we hear the imprecatory or cursing note which recurs in the psalms, and which I examined further in the Introduction. As elsewhere, we cannot simply omit these verses. We need to read them as part of the whole.

Jubilation

There is a strong personal note in verses 1–3 and in 6–7, a note of jubilation in God. The psalmist wants to celebrate the God who has answered his prayers (v. 6) and who is his 'strength and shield', the focus of his trust and the source of his joy (v. 7). How much more central should celebration be for us who are the Easter people and the Pentecost people! 'Lift up your hearts,' says the President at the eucharist (the word, of course, means thanksgiving). 'We lift them to the Lord,' we say. 'Let us give thanks to the Lord our God,' he says. 'It is right to give him thanks and praise,' we cry.

In verses 8 and 9, the psalmist looks away from himself to his nation and to its leader ('his anointed one'—see 20:6 and note). He ends his psalm with a prayer for them all, as we find at the end of Psalm 25 (v. 22). A nation built on rock will not fall when rain comes and floods rise, and winds blow and batter against the house (see Matthew 7:24–27).

Let us ADORE

Dear name! the rock on which I build,
My shield and hiding place,
My never-failing treasury filled
With boundless stores of grace.

Jesus! my Shepherd, Brother, Friend,
My Prophet, Priest and King,
My Lord, my Life, my Way, my End,
Accept the praise I bring.

John Newton (1725–1807)

GOD *of the* STORM

This psalmist knew how to handle language. Is there in all the Bible a more terrifying description of a storm than the one he gives us here? He is concerned to convey to us some idea of the 'glory and might' of God (v. 1). He decides to use nature at its wildest to illustrate his theme. Through nature the Lord makes his voice heard—'the voice of the Lord' comes seven times in this brief psalm. There is power in repetition.

Verse 3 tells of 'the waters'—seas were always menacing to the Hebrew, as we have seen in Psalm 24—and how the Lord 'thunders' —mysterious language and reminiscent of Sinai (see, for example, Exodus 19:16). We read of the desert storm which whips up the sand in swirling gusts and blots out vision: 'the voice of the Lord makes the wilderness writhe in travail, the Lord makes the wilderness of Kadesh writhe' (v. 8). We hear of the terror which makes the cattle give birth prematurely, and leaves behind a trail of destruction (v. 9). No imagery is spared. We can almost hear the crash—and tremble!

God's people at worship

But the primary aim of the psalmist is not to terrify his audience. Another picture is in his mind. In the temple, God's people are at worship, 'in holy attire' (v. 2) worshipping the Lord. Storms may rage, destruction may increase, but God has not lost control of his world— he is 'above the flood and has taken his seat as king for ever' (v. 10). Nor is he a remote potentate, unconcerned for the welfare of mere mortals. He desires a people strong and at peace—he 'will give strength to his people; the Lord will bless his people with peace' (v. 11).

Who are the 'angelic powers' (v. 1)? The original Hebrew words mean 'sons of the gods'. It is hard to say. Perhaps it is the angels who are conceived of as constituting the heavenly court, suitably attired ('...in holy attire', v. 1) and engaged in divine worship. We find similar expressions—'the assembly of the angels... court of heaven... the council of the angels'—in Psalm 89:5–7. They are a kind of model for those on earth who carry on the never-ceasing activity of adoration and praise.

MEDITATION

*As I looked I heard, all round the throne and the living creatures
and the elders, the voices of many angels, thousands on thousands,
myriads on myriads. They proclaimed with loud voices:
'Worthy is the Lamb who was slain, to receive power and wealth,
wisdom and might, honour and glory and praise!'
Then I heard all created things, in heaven, on earth, under the
earth, and in the sea, crying:
'Praise and honour, glory and might, to him who sits on the throne
and to the Lamb for ever!'*

Revelation 5:11–13

PSALM 30

BLUE SKIES

The sun was out that morning for the man who wrote this psalm. The sky was mostly blue; what clouds there were came from recalling former days when things had gone hard for him. It had not always been easy. There had been enemies (v. 1), sickness (v. 2), times when he faced God's anger, nights when tears lingered: 'In his anger is distress, in his favour there is life. Tears may linger at nightfall, but rejoicing comes in the morning' (v. 5). There had been days when God's face was hidden from him (v. 7), periods of lamentation and sackcloth (v. 11). He does not linger over these things; he mentions them—they are the rough passages of life which form part of the experience of all human beings. When handled as this man handles them, they may become constituent parts of a strong and godly character.

The brevity of life

There was one other thing which constituted a sombre element in his experience. It was the consciousness of the brevity and fragility of life and the fear of death and of what he calls Sheol, the place of darkness (v. 3). After death, what? He has little positive to say. For him, it could best be hinted at as 'the abyss' (v. 3), 'the pit' where there is an end to praising God and to proclaiming his truth (v. 9). 'Can the dust praise you? Can it proclaim your truth?' He puts it in question form, but I do not detect much sign of hope. The strong clear note of death as a gate to fuller life was to wait till he came who was 'the resurrection and the life' (John 11:25).

But our psalmist knows a great deal about God. He knows him as saviour (vv. 1, 3), as healer (v. 2), as one who makes his 'mountain strong' (v. 7; what did he mean by that?), as one who made him dance for joy: 'You have turned my laments into dancing; you have stripped off my sackcloth and clothed me with joy' (v. 11). So he learns to *adore* his God—to exalt him (v. 1), to sing a psalm and give thanks to him (v. 4), to praise him for ever (v. 12).

True worship

'Worship,' said Archbishop William Temple, 'is the submission of all our nature to God. It is the quickening of conscience by his holiness; the nourishment of mind with his truth; the purifying of imagination by his beauty; the opening of the heart to his love; the surrender of will to his purposes—and all of this gathered up in *adoration*, the most selfless emotion of which our nature is capable, and therefore the chief remedy for that self-centredness which is our original sin and the source of all actual sin' (from *Readings in St John's Gospel*, 1939).

Let us WORSHIP

I shall exalt you, Lord.
Lord my God, I shall praise you for ever.
O come, let us adore him.

VISION & HOPE, DESPAIR & DOUBT

This psalm is like a spring day, a mixture of sunshine and shadow, the one chasing the other—in and out. It is good that it is part of the Psalter, for certainly this is part of life experience for most of us. In the spiritual life, too, we have our bright days of vision and hope, and our darker ones of despair and doubt.

It would seem that our psalmist's distress is two-fold—there are causes which are physical and mental, perhaps nervous (vv. 9, 10): 'My life is worn away with sorrow and my years with sighing' (v. 10). There are enemies who scorn him, threatening, conspiring, scheming —even his neighbours find him burdensome (vv. 11–13): 'For I hear many whispering threats from every side conspiring against me and scheming to take my life' (v. 13). But the sun wins in the end (vv. 19–22): 'How great is your goodness, stored up for those who fear you, made manifest before mortal eyes for all who turn to you for shelter' (v. 19). God has a fund of goodness, a store of grace awaiting our exploration and acceptance. He is a rock of refuge, as we read in Psalm 28.

Unfailing love

No wonder, then, that the psalm ends with the writer's testimony to the Lord's unfailing love (vv. 21, 22) and with an appeal to others to return that love and live a life strong and full of hope (vv. 23, 24). We shall see a similar appeal in Psalm 34:8ff.

It was a verse from this psalm (v. 5) which Jesus used as the last of his seven words from the cross, prefacing it with his usual address of 'Father' (Luke 23:46). Was he saying the opening words of this psalm to himself in his agony? The awful cry 'My God, my God, why have you forsaken me?' is past, and now, as the end draws near, he can say, as our psalmist did (v. 8), 'you have not abandoned me', and he can die in peace.

If your Bible includes the Apocrypha, it would be worthwhile to read Ecclesiasticus 2. In *Celebrating Common Prayer*, it is set as one of the Lessons for the Eve of St Thomas' Day (July 3), that splendid man who doubted and won through. 'My son', it begins, 'if you aspire to be a servant of the Lord, prepare yourself for testing...' Endurance is a key word of the New Testament. As we saw in reading Psalm 13, the word is often translated as 'patience', but is much more than that. It has about it the sense of fortitude, steadfastness, endurance. Paul speaks of 'the steadfastness of Christ'; he sees it as one of the constituent words of that unique character (2 Thessalonians 3:5). There is much of this steady holding-on-until-the-sun-comes-out in this psalm. The Rock will not move.

PRAYER

May the Lord direct our hearts towards God's love and the steadfastness of Christ.

Be strong and stout-hearted, all you whose hope is in the Lord.

31

The POWER of FORGIVENESS

The psalmist has been ill with a wasting disease. The nights have brought him no relief as he tosses on his bed with a raging temperature (vv. 3, 4). His suffering has been all the greater because he saw it as the result of his own sin. He does not say what was the nature of that sin—was it perhaps a wrong relationship with someone else, a lack of forgiveness on his part towards someone who had wronged him? At last, he knows what to do—perhaps he knew all along. He will make a clean breast of it—he will no longer conceal his guilt, he will confess his sin to the Lord (v. 5). God has been there all along—a 'hiding-place', a 'guard', longing to 'enfold him in salvation' (v. 7), in 'unfailing love' (v. 10). He can be happy again (v. 1) and the language here reminds us of the happy man of Psalm 1: 'Happy is the one who does not take the counsel of the wicked for a guide' (Psalm 1:1). What a relief! Forgiveness is the most therapeutic power in the world.

Now he hears the patient voice of God—'I shall teach you... guide you... keep you under my eye' (v. 8). But please don't be obstinate, like some senseless mule who will not respond to restraint and only hurts itself by kicking against the goad (we might recall the story of Saul's conversion in Acts 26:14). Don't keep up a controversy with God. Keep short accounts with him—it is an unfailing recipe for a happy conscience and a life at peace. Would 'don't be a silly ass' be too free a translation for the first half of verse 9?

Sharing the joy

I see verses 8 and 9 as the speech of God and verses 10 and 11 as the psalmist's exhortation to any who will listen. His sin confessed and forgiven, he can feel God's forgiveness enfolding him and setting him on his feet. He cannot keep this to himself—he must share his joy with others: 'Many are the torments for the ungodly, but unfailing love enfolds those who trust in the Lord' (v. 10).

Evangelism has been defined as 'one beggar telling another beggar where to find bread'. That is a good definition. Our psalmist might have said that evangelism is 'one sick person telling another sick person where to find forgiveness'. That's good, too. But *all* the

Christian basics are good. Why are we so slow in responding? 'Rejoice in the Lord and be glad, you righteous ones; sing aloud, all you of honest heart' (v. 11).

PRAYER

As your living word
brings light out of darkness, O Lord,
so may your Spirit renew the face of the earth,
bending our wills to the gentle rule of your love,
now and for ever.

Celebrating Common Prayer

The POWER of MUSIC

This is the first mention so far in the Psalter of music as part of Israel's worship. We shall frequently be reminded of it as we work our way through the rest of the psalms (for example Psalm 57:8; 108:1–2). The last psalm in the book introduces us to a veritable orchestra (Psalm 150:3–5).

God has a way of reaching people through music, and not only by the spoken word. In a passage in his *Confessions*, Augustine describes his baptism and that of his son, Adeodatus. In the days that followed, he was considering the profundity of God's purpose for the salvation of the human race. 'I was deeply moved by the music of the sweet chants of your Church... The sounds flowed into my ears and the truth was distilled into my heart.' There are multitudes today who could echo these words. Often the words of a hymn linger longer than the words of a sermon. The creation of great works of sacred music has been one of the major responses of humanity to the outgoing grace and beauty of God. To foster and encourage good music to the glory of God and thereby to commend his truth and loveliness to others is one of the noblest tasks to which human beings can aspire.

God's word at work

In verses 4 and 6 the writer touches on one of the major themes of scripture—the 'word of the Lord'. His language reminds us of the creation stories in Genesis and especially the first one (Genesis 1:3–2:3) in which God is depicted as uttering his *word* with the result that darkness gave way to light and chaos to order. God is no inscrutable sphinx looking down in silence on his world. He declares himself and his purposes. He speaks, and his word has creative power. The theme recurs again and again—in the messages of the prophets who bore God's word to people; in the Wisdom literature of the Bible books and of the Apocrypha; in the activity of Jesus in his healing work (see, for example, Matthew 8:1–16, noting specially verses 8 and 16: 'But the centurion replied, "Sir, I am not worthy to have you under my roof. You need only say the word and my servant will be cured"... That evening they brought to him many who were possessed by demons; and he drove the spirits out with a word and healed all who were sick'; and, supremely, in the Prologue to John's Gospel (John 1:1–18, itself echoing the Genesis creation story). In the Gospel the Word of God is no longer an utterance; it is a flesh and blood person. 'The Word became flesh; he made his home among us, and we saw his glory.'

Moreover, God has a purpose, a plan, for his creation, a plan which will endure—he will see it through to its completion: 'The Lord frustrates the purposes of nations; he foils the plans of the peoples. But the Lord's own purpose stands for ever, and the plans he has in mind endure for all generations' (vv. 10, 11). This again is a theme which runs through scripture and reaches its climax in such a passage as Ephesians 1:9–10. Here Paul marvels that the plan has been made known in Christ; it will be put into effect when the time is ripe. What is it? 'That the universe, everything in heaven and on earth', will 'be brought into a unity in Christ'. God will not be defeated. 'For in him [Christ] God in all his fulness chose to dwell, and through him to reconcile all things to himself, making peace through the shedding of his blood on the cross—all things, whether on earth or in heaven' (Colossians 1:19–20). That is the basis of the Christian hope.

To PONDER

Let hope keep you joyful;
In trouble stand firm.

Romans 12:12

WITNESS & INVITATION

The writer of this psalm has found in his religion something infinitely good. God has made himself known to him in a wonderfully gracious way. He cannot keep this to himself. He must share it with his friends. So this psalm is both a *witness* to what God has done for him and means to him, and an *invitation* to others to share his experience.

His witness is clear: God has heard his prayers and set him free (vv. 4, 6, 10 and others). His invitation is sincere; he calls on others to join him in worship: 'Glorify the Lord with me; let us exalt his name together' (v. 3). He calls them to join in tasting and seeing (v. 8), in listening and learning (v. 11).

'Taste and see'. There is a feast of good things awaiting us. Nobody else can do the tasting on our behalf. We ourselves must do the sampling of God's supplies. Many good people miss the joy of the Christian faith because they have never taken the risk, sampled the food, responded to the invitation. To change the metaphor, they have dipped their toes in the sea, but never jumped in to prove that the water will carry them. I believe that God is on the side of the questing mind; but there comes a time when, in an act of committal, we jump in, doubts and all, in an act of faith and trust. In worship with God's people (v. 3), in humble willingness to listen and be taught (v. 11), there will be a steady growth in 'the fear of the Lord' (v. 11). As we saw in Psalm 25, 'fear' carries with it the sense of 'reverence'. We are not called to be scared of God, but to seek to honour him in all we do.

In v. 10, 'Princes'—the word means 'young lions'—may be a metaphor for 'leaders'. Position in society does not of itself bring satisfaction. 'Those who seek the Lord lack no good thing'; they have inner, unseen resources on which to draw.

For 'Keep your tongue' (v. 13), see Psalm 12 and note; James 3:1–12 should be re-read.

Finding satisfaction

Our psalmist writes as a satisfied man; not self-satisfied, but satisfied in the God who was revealing himself to him. He knows where to slake his thirst, where to find his nourishment. Isaiah, in a moving passage, sees his people on the search for satisfaction—where can they find water, food, nourishment? They will pay anything that is asked. The prophet will show them. Are they thirsty for water? He will show them wine and milk! What shall they pay? Not a cent! God's offer is *gratis*, grace, from a lavish hand. 'Listen to me... come to me... hear me and you will have life' (Isaiah 55:1–3). And in the New Testament we read how 'on the last and greatest day of the festival Jesus stood and declared, "If anyone is thirsty, let him come to me and drink. Whoever believes in me, as Scripture says, 'Streams of living water shall flow from within him'"' (John 7:37, 38). The one who comes to the Christ will find not only that his own needs are met but also that he is able to meet the needs of others—God's grace overflows, through him.

We have a generous God. Taste and see that he is good.

INVITATION

Read and ponder Isaiah 55:1–3 and John 7:37, 38. Note that the promised satisfaction is not for selfish purposes—'streams of living water shall flow from within him' (John 7:38) for the blessing of others.

BEGGING *for* VENGEANCE

This psalm presents us with a man who feels himself to have been deeply wronged—undeservedly wronged. It is an urgent cry to God for vengeance on these enemies: God is invited—in very human language!—to 'grasp shield and buckler', to 'brandish spear and axe' (vv. 2, 3) against them, and there is a broad and angry suggestion that God has been dilatory and it is high time he roused himself (vv. 22, 23): 'Awake, rouse yourself, my God, my Lord' (v. 23). The prayer for his enemies' destruction is detailed in verses 4–8. The psalm is a very unhappy piece of writing, to say the least. The psalmist cannot get his enemies out of his mind. The memory of them is like a recurring bad dream. They prey on him (v. 10); they malign him (v. 11); they lie in wait for him (v. 12); they gloat over his fall (v. 15), and so on.

The trouble with this psalm is that it is so true to life! All of us get injured—hurt by people who we thought were our friends. The question is: *What do we do with our hurts?* Some people nurse them, recall them and, maybe, exaggerate them. 'I'm not on speaking terms with X,' they say, recalling some incident of years gone by. So the wound festers, and poisons the blood of relationships. Jeremiah heard *God* say about people who had injured *him*: 'Their sin I shall call to mind no more' (Jeremiah 31:34). That is the divine reaction—God the great Forgetter! But, we say, that wound has left an indelible mark. That may be true.

Indelible scars

But that does not mean that we can do nothing about it. We can determine not to dwell on the wrong done to us. We can pray for those who injured us, as Jesus taught us to do (Matthew 5:44). When we recall the injury, we can learn to switch off, to turn to another programme, and to 'fill our thoughts... with all that is true, noble, just and pure, all that is loveable and attractive, excellent and admirable' (Philippians 4:8). And our psalmist himself, though he seems to postpone it until he has been vindicated, gives us a hint which undoubtedly would help us in the present—praising God, extolling him, in the presence of his people, in corporate worship (vv. 18, 28). This lifts the soul, gives a sense of proportion to life, and raises us from the contemplation of our griefs to the wonder of his presence.

I wrote above about 'indelible' scars, the marks left after a wound has been healed. Winston Churchill, speaking in *national* terms, referred to 'honourable scars', the marks that the cities of Britain bore as a result of the Nazi bombings. There are such things in personal life. Men and women can be finer persons for the scars that they bear. They have been tried and tested, and this has lefts its marks. But surrendered to God's re-creative power, they can be honourable scars. Indeed, they could become 'the marks of the Lord Jesus' (Galatians 6:17). The wound has long ceased to suppurate. Those who bear the scars are no longer bitter about the incident. God has handled the misery of it all, as they have brought it to him. He has healed the memory, and they are free. Why should this not be true in your case?

There are indications that the psalmist has not got as far as this in his religious experience. He remains an angry man. But then he had no knowledge of the One who 'when he was abused... did not retaliate, when he suffered he offered no threats, but delivered himself up to him who judges justly' (1 Peter 2:23).

To PONDER

What is meant by 'the glorious liberty of the children of God'?
(Romans 8:21)

A BIG SUBJECT

An artist who wants to paint an object of great beauty will often set it against a dark background. He knows that the darker the background, the more clear will be the colours of his object. A crimson flower against a pitch-black curtain—the scene is set.

The writer of this psalm has seen something of the wonder of God. In rich colours he depicts God's unfailing love, his faithfulness (v. 5), his righteousness, his justice (v. 6). The subject is too big for him— he calls on the skies, the mountains, the great deep to help him in his task (vv. 5, 6). His colours are rich and strong.

The godless and the fountain of life

For the background of his picture, he describes the person to whom all this is totally irrelevant. It means nothing at all. His conscience is seared, his judgments distorted. Even when his iniquity is found out, it involves for him no changes in the course of his conduct (v. 2). His godlessness is reflected in his speech (vv. 1, 3). He has no sense of right or wrong. The background is black indeed. The contrast is stark.

But there are others who have spurned the way of godlessness. They are open to the graciousness of God. They have found the fountain of life. They are constantly enriched by God's plenty, their dryness watered by his never-failing streams. They know the Light of the world (vv. 7–9): 'for with you is the fountain of life, and by your light we are enlightened' (v. 9).

Paul attempts the same theme in three powerful verses in his letter to the Romans (6:12–14). He depicts someone who matches the character sketched in the opening verses of our psalm—his powers put at sin's disposal. By way of contrast, he depicts another who has taken the step of putting all *his* powers at the disposal of God—he has been raised from death to life, his body yielded to God as an implement for doing right. No longer is he mastered by sin. He is free—to live open to all the goodness of God.

A psalm of contrast

Psalm 36 is a psalm of contrast. 'Which course is yours?' the psalmist would seem to ask the reader. 'It's up to you to decide.'

The psalm ends with a prayer (vv. 10, 11). God's resources are at his disposal. All can be well. God's love is unfailing, his saving power always at the ready. One final glance at 'the evildoers' (v. 12) is enough to warn him. 'If you think you are standing firm, take care, or you may fall' (1 Corinthians 10:12).

Let us PRAISE

Long my imprisoned spirit lay
Fast bound in sin and nature's night;
Thine eye diffused a quickening ray—
I woke, the dungeon flamed with light.
My chains fell off, my heart was free,
I rose, went forth, and followed thee.

Charles Wesley (1707–88)

UNFAIR—*or is it?*

This psalmist is wrestling with a problem: life is unfair; why do the wicked so often get away with it? The question rumbles on throughout the long psalm, like thunder in the distance on a calm evening. The writer's exhortations *not* to be vexed, *not* to envy (vv. 1, 7), *not* to get hot and bothered (v. 8) only reflect his own reactions to the problem. Unless some light is thrown on it, he himself will be a damaged man. He says he is old, yet he has never seen the righteous forsaken or their children begging their bread (v. 25). We are tempted to reply that he cannot have looked very far—anyone with their eyes open can see instance after instance!

Let us be honest: we all wrestle with this problem. They are wise people who admit that there is likely to be *no* adequate answer to it in this life, though there is light on it. The final answer must await the day of judgment, 'when the secrets of all hearts shall be disclosed'. That is the point where our psalmist is so much less fortunate than we are: he has virtually no doctrine of an after-life. Death for him means *Sheol*, shades, darkness, as we noted in reading Psalm 6. As we say together in the Nicene creed: 'We look for the resurrection of the dead, and the life of the world to come'. We have a perspective on the problem which was denied to him. Jesus taught about a treasure-store in heaven (Matthew 6:19) and Paul about unseen things which are eternal in contrast to those which are seen and transient (2 Corinthians 4:18). The dimension of eternity, while it does not solve the problem, helps, and adds a sense of seriousness and responsibility to everyday living.

The Lord's watchful care

Even so, the psalmist has much to offer. He is conscious of the upholding presence of the Lord and of his watchful care (vv. 17, 18). Few possessions and a happy conscience is better than wealth and an uneasy one (v. 16). Adopting God's values as our own is a source of well-being. Character matters more than bank balance.

There is another way of approaching this psalm. It is to take the psalmist as our spiritual director, and to heed his injunctions and live by them. He gives a series of directives for the unembittered life:

- *Negatively*, don't be envious of the wicked (vv. 1, 7); don't get hot under the collar (v. 8). The godly have spiritual treasures beyond price of which the ungodly know nothing.

- *Positively*, trust in the Lord (vv. 3, 5b); delight in the Lord (v. 4); commit your way to the Lord (v. 5); wait quietly for the Lord (vv. 7, 34)

To PONDER

Think about those four positive injunctions over the next four days, one each day. It will enrich your spiritual life.

The BRINK *of* DISASTER

It would be interesting to see what a doctor, or for that matter, a psy-chiatrist, would make of this psalm. Clearly, the writer is in a very bad way physically—his 'whole frame' is involved (v. 3). Was his disease infectious?—his friends and relations kept at a distance (v. 11). The wording of this psalm describing the writer's plight is very similar to, though more detailed than, that of Psalm 6. It would be helpful to re-read the comment on that psalm. In the mind of the psalmist, there is the same linking of his sickness with the anger of God at his sin. This exacerbates his grief. And there is anxiety as to his future—he feels that he is 'on the brink of disaster' (v. 17). Is this psalmist a man whose guilty conscience keeps nagging at him?

There is much suffering which is the result, direct or indirect, of human sin. But to make the assertion that 'I am ill, therefore God must be angry with me' is, surely, far from the truth. It is to think of a God who pulls the rug from under our feet, who trips us up. This is not the God of our Lord and Saviour Jesus Christ, and it is incumbent on us to do what we can to put paid to such a picture of him.

Wholeness and holiness

God is on the side of health, of wholeness, of holiness. One of the things which made Christianity so appealing to the ancient world was its healing work. The healing work of Jesus was one of the signs that the Kingdom of God had come upon the people, and 'the apostolic band saw their work as involving the continuation of his ministry among the sick; for healing the sick was at once a proclamation of the presence of God's Kingdom, and at the same time a sign that Satan, the source of all sickness and mental confusion, was challenged and overcome'. That is a quotation from Christopher Donaldson's *Martin of Tours*, a book which makes it abundantly clear that Martin regarded the healing ministry as part and parcel of his work as a bishop.

We return to our psalmist. He is a sorry sight, physically and nervously crushed. But his faith in God has not wholly gone. He is not totally forsaken. He does not cry out, as did the author of Psalm 22, 'My God, my God, why *have* you *forsaken* me?' He can still plead, '*Do not forsake me*' (v. 21). God is still the centre of his hope; he is the

God who answers prayer (v. 15). He is his 'deliverer' (v. 22). The psalmist will hang on to his Rock even if it is by his fingernails. Such faith, even though it may be as small as a grain of mustard seed, is mighty.

THANK GOD

Great is thy faithfulness, O God my Father,
There is no shadow of turning with thee;
Thou changest not, thy compassions they fail not;
As thou hast been thou for ever wilt be.

Thomas Chisholm (1866–1960)

38 PSALM 39

LIFE'S BREVITY

'... A muzzle on my mouth... I kept utterly silent, I refrained from speech'. Wise man! Words are sacred things. We should not waste them. There is a place for silence and for the discipline of restraint. Too often we blurt something out and live to regret it. There is no recall to the spoken word (vv. 1, 2).

But at last the psalmist speaks and his words are sad. He is oppressed by the dark cloud of life's brevity and fragility. 'A human being... is but a puff of wind' (v. 5), 'a passing shadow' (v. 6). All too soon he will 'depart and cease to be' (v. 13)—here today and gone tomorrow. Not only is there this ever-present dark cloud, but there is also the haunting sense of divine hostility (v. 10), of God's frown on him (v. 13).

People of the psalmist's generation thought themselves lucky if they reached the great age of seventy (the proverbial three score years and ten), luckier still if they made eighty (Psalm 90:10). The labours of modern scientists have given us an extra decade or two to play with. Play with? Our psalmist faces us with a problem which is *always* present to the thinking person: life with all its fragility and brevity—what do we do with it? *Time*—how do we use it? 'Killing time' we say. But surely that is 'murder most foul'. Time as a loan from God, to be used to the full, and enjoyed to the full—that's better. Time used with God's smile on us and then, the brief span completed, death—not 'ceasing to be' (v. 13) but the gate to glory. That's best of all. So we come to terms with life's transitoriness, and are not oppressed by it.

A word of cheer

In spite of the psalmist's black cloud as he surveys life's brevity and his haunting sense of God's hostility, he manages to utter a word of cheer: 'Now, Lord, what do I wait for? My hope is in you' (v. 7). Hope is a close cousin to faith. Hope is faith looking forward. And faith is the conviction that God can be trusted and the willingness to bet your life on it. The writer of the letter to the Hebrews speaks of a hope which is 'an anchor for our lives, safe and secure' (Hebrews 6:19). For that we can thank God. From that we can take courage. By that we can live responsible lives.

A THOUGHT

Redeem thy mis-spent time that's past,
And live this day as if thy last;
Improve thy talent with due care;
For the great day thyself prepare.

A PRAYER

Direct, control, suggest, this day,
All I design or do or say;
That all my powers, with all their might,
In thy sole glory may unite.

Bishop Thomas Ken (1637–1710)

SPIRITUAL AUTOBIOGRAPHY

This is a very personal psalm, a piece of spiritual autobiography. The writer is good enough to share with us his experience of God in public life (v. 9), in misfortune and sinful behaviour (v. 12), in spiritual elation and joy (v. 3ff). I find the reading of biography and autobiography a very fruitful activity. It humbles us when we are tempted to be swollen-headed. It stimulates us when our discipleship is flagging: if God can do this in the case of X, he might do it in my case.

Everything in this psalm depends on the opening verse: 'Patiently I waited for the Lord; he bent down to me and listened to my cry' (v. 1). The psalmist's God is one who *bends down and listens*. We too must listen. God can only be heard when, at the receiving end, we 'patiently wait' for him. The Hebrew is interesting—'waiting I waited'. Only then do things happen.

'The miry pit, the mud and clay...' (v. 2). What was this, I wonder? Was it 'the slippery paths of youth' when he ran 'with heedless steps'—were these the formative years when so easily he might have taken the wrong turn and messed up his life for ever? It was a great day when God stepped in and set his feet on rock and gave him a firm footing. Henceforth he was a man with a song on his lips (v. 3), with the secret of true happiness in his heart (v. 4). Words are poor things when he tries to put his experience into mere prose (v. 5), but the song on his lips and the genuineness of his faith were noticed and led to others putting their trust in the Lord (v. 3).

True sacrifice

In verses 6–11 the psalmist invites us to enter fully into a discovery he has made. He had been brought up in a religion which gave enormous importance to animal sacrifice. Every morning and evening, and especially at the great annual feasts, the slaughter went on, and the animal sacrifices were offered. But was this really what God desired? The question tantalized and troubled him. He found himself asking: Is not real religion more a matter of attention ('receptive ears', v. 6), an inner passion to do God's will (v. 8), a matter of the 'heart'? The Old Testament prophets often expressed their dis-ease with the sacrificial system. Amos 5:21 is a case in point: 'I spurn with loathing your pilgrim-feasts; I take no pleasure in your sacred ceremonies.' Hearing the word of God and obeying the demands of an educated conscience seemed to them the truer religion than the offering of endless sacrifices. The same theme is dealt with by the author of the epistle to the Hebrews in 10:5–10; not whole-offerings, but 'Here I am... I have come to do your will'. That being so, our psalmist *has a gospel to proclaim* and, as a leader in the community, declare it he will (vv. 9, 10)—he simply cannot 'conceal' God's 'unfailing love and truth'. As Peter and John were to say, when threatened by the authorities and forbidden to preach: 'We cannot possibly give up speaking about what we have seen and heard' (Acts 4:20).

Discipleship of this listening God (v. 1) does not mean that we are exempt from trouble, nor promise us a life-long bed of roses. The closing verses of the psalm (vv. 12–17) introduce us to rough passages in the writer's experience. Within, his own iniquities, more in number than the hairs of his head, have blinded him (v. 12). Without, his enemies seek his life and rejoice at his downfall (vv. 14–15). But he knows where to go when he is in disgrace or in peril. The Lord is his help and deliverer (v. 17). The listening God is his rock (vv. 1, 2).

To PONDER

'I said, "Here I am"... God, my desire is to do your will' (vv. 7, 8).

The Virgin Mary receives the Son of God, in order to give that Son away to all humanity. It is the same with the Church. She receives the means of grace, the Word of God, the sacraments, etc., in order precisely to pass on or give them away.

Chiara Lubich (in Jim Gallacher, *A Woman's Work*)

GOD *as a* NURSE

'Happy is anyone who has a concern for the helpless!' (v. 1). One of the encouraging facets of life in the West today is the public response which is generated when a national disaster occurs or a special need presents itself. Radio, TV and the press go into action, and millions of pounds pour in. It is spasmodic giving, and reflects no planning, still less tithing, on the part of the givers. And we are still *insular* in the thinking behind our giving, and the needs of the developing countries far exceed those of our own. But 'happy is anyone who has a concern for the helpless', wherever they may be.

God as a *nurse* (v. 3)—it is a daring concept. But we need not be surprised at this tender touch, for both Old and New Testaments speak of a God who wipes away human tears from our eyes: 'He will destroy death for ever. Then the Lord God will wipe away the tears from every face, and throughout the world remove the indignities from his people. The Lord has spoken' (Isaiah 25:8). 'The Lamb who is at the centre of the throne will be their shepherd and will guide them to springs of the water of life; and God will wipe every tear from their eyes' (Revelation 7:17). 'He will wipe every tear from their eyes. There shall be an end to death, and to mourning and crying and pain, for the old order has passed away!' (Revelation 21:4).

Sin and sickness

Verses 4–12 present us with a little drama: the *psalmist* himself is in conversation with his God. He is conscious of his sin (v. 4) which he links with his sickness: 'I said "Lord, be gracious to me! Heal me, for I have sinned against you"' (v. 4). On this, see also Psalm 6 and comment.

Then there are *his enemies*. We can see them gloating over the psalmist's fall, rubbing their hands in glee as they contemplate his imminent death (v. 5); visiting him, but only in order to have ground for spreading the good news that he is soon to die—he is under an evil spell (v. 8). Worst of all is the treachery of a friend whom he had always trusted (v. 9). That is 'the most unkindest cut of all'.

Then there is *God*. The enemies seem to have forgotten that this is a *godly* man. To God he can turn for restoration of health (even though the motive of his prayer is not of the highest—'that I may repay them in full'!). He serves the God of grace, who is deeply concerned to restore his servant to health (vv. 4, 10). The enemies may have forgotten, but the psalmist has not. He knows he is upheld by God, kept for ever in his presence (v. 12). That is enough to steady him. Faithful is God who has called him. He can trust and not be afraid.

Verse 13 provides a formal ending to book I of the series of five books which make up the Psalter (see Introduction). For similar endings see 72:18–20; 89:52; 106:48; 150:6.

PRAYER

O God, gather me now
to be with you
as you are with me.
Soothe my tiredness;
quiet my fretfulness;
curb my aimlessness;
relieve my compulsiveness;
Let me be easy for a moment.

From Ted Loder, *Guerillas of Grace*

41 PSALMS 42 AND 43

FAR *from* HOME

Psalms 42 and 43 are so obviously one that we might wonder how it was that they ever got separated. There is a unity of *desire*, of longing for God, of regret and yet of hope; and there is a unity of *refrain* which binds them together—'how deep I am sunk in misery, groaning in my distress! I shall wait for God; I shall yet praise him, my deliverer, my God' (Psalm 42:5, 11; 43:5).

Let us get the picture clear in our minds, the life-situation which gave birth to this psalm. The writer is away from home, living in the far north, near where the Jordan rises (v. 6, Mount Hermon; the exact location of Mizar is unknown). He is unable, perhaps because of sickness, to join his people on their visits to the temple at Jerusalem. Cataracts... waves... breakers of depression sweep over him (v. 7) when he recalls the temple where he used to worship. The very thought of it brought tears to his eyes. Those were the days!—the days of marches in the ranks of the great to God's house, the shouts of praise, the music, the noisy clamour of the pilgrims as they trudged up the ascent to the house of God at the great annual feasts...

The psalmist is tempted to wallow in the misery of regret and self-pity (v. 6)—he feels that God has forgotten him (v. 9, see also 22:1)—despair and dereliction are a dire couple of visitors to anyone. The beauty of it all—and now *this*!

Regrets and thankfulness

Was he an *old* man, this writer? We have all met his successors—their every other sentence beginning with a sigh and 'I remember...' We must spare them a thought and a place in our sympathy, for regret must accompany retrospect in any honest person's life. But we have all met their opposite numbers, as well. Yes, they look back but their regrets are tempered by thankfulness: how good God has been! How great were the privileges of those halcyon days: corporate worship, friendships without number, work so worthwhile! Sheer thankfulness drives out the mists of regret. With the psalmist in his better moments, they say: 'I shall yet praise him, my deliverer, my God' (v. 11). 'By day the Lord grants his unfailing love; at night his praise is upon my lips...' (v. 8).

The psalm opens with the vivid picture of the hind (the female deer) longing for the running streams. She runs, sniffing for the slightest scent of water. Her very life depends on her finding it. The thought is elaborated in the three-fold refrain: 'I shall wait for God' (Psalm 42:5, 11; 43:5). Human beings waiting for God are human beings at their best—thirsty for God, his will, his strength, his peace.

When Jesus hung on the cross, John recounts that 'Jesus, aware that all had now come to its appointed end, said in fulfilment of scripture, "I am thirsty."' (John 19:28). Of course he was thirsty. The sun was beating down on his body. The pain was excruciating. Oh, for a drink! But I think there was a deeper meaning to that cry, deeper than physical thirst. He was thirsty for *God*. He was thirsty to do his will even to the point of death. That had been his motto throughout life. 'Here I am... ; I have come, O God, to do your will' (Hebrews 10:7). It would be his motto to the end.

MEDITATION

Late have I loved you, beauty so old and so new: late have I loved you... You were fragrant, and I drew in my breath and now pant after you. I tasted you, and I feel but hunger and thirst for you. You touched me, and I am set on fire to attain the peace that is yours.

Augustine, *Confessions*

Almighty God, in whom we live and move and have our being and who hast made us for thyself, so that our hearts are restless till they rest in thee: Grant us purity of heart and strength of purpose, that no selfish passion may hinder us from knowing thy will, no weakness from doing it, but that in thy light we may see light clearly, and in thy service find perfect freedom; through Jesus Christ our Lord.

The LESSONS of HISTORY

'We have heard for ourselves... our forefathers have told us...' (v. 1). Indeed they had! Generation after generation the stories had been repeated—round the camp-fires, in the houses of the people, and (later) in the synagogues. The stories had been told and re-told, each generation adding its bit—stories of Noah and his ark, of Moses and his teaching, of the judges and their (often bloody) exploits, of David and his valour (and his lusts), of Solomon and his wisdom (and his wives: it was said he had seven hundred of them, 'all princesses, and three hundred concubines', 1 Kings 11:3). The 'forefathers' loved to tell the stories, and the people loved to hear, to add, to remember. One of the most powerful verbs of the Old Testament is the verb to *remember*, to recall, to learn the lessons of history.

For Israel's God was the God who *acts* on the stage of human history, often using the most unlikely agents for the pursuit of his purposes. Even a tyrant like Cyrus can be called his 'shepherd', his 'anointed'—see Isaiah 44:28 and 45:1. Our psalmist sees God's 'hand', his 'strong arm', his 'presence' at work in planting his people in their own land and in driving out the 'nations' to make room for them (vv. 2, 3).

Plant in the land

'To *plant* them in the land' (v. 2). This is a favourite simile in describing God's relationship to his people Israel. One of the best instances is the little love-song of Isaiah 5:1–7. With immense care, God prepares the land, plants it with the choicest vines, and in high hopes waits for a bumper crop. All that appears is 'a crop of wild grapes', to the vast disappointment of the owner. 'The vineyard of the Lord of Hosts is Israel... He looked for justice but found bloodshed, for righteousness but heard cries of distress' (v. 7).

As the author of this psalm looks back over Israel's history and of God's activity within it, his confidence in God is renewed—there is a note of strong assurance in verses 4 to 8.

Awake!

But it is not all sunshine. The clouds gather in verses 9 to 16. Little Israel has been in retreat, plundered at the will of its enemies, exposed to gibes and mocking—the rigmarole of misery goes on. Meanwhile, God appears to have been asleep, and the psalmist, greatly daring, calls on God to wake up! (v. 23). He points out (as though God needed to be reminded!) that he himself and his people have not forgotten him—had they done so, the all-knowing God would certainly have found out (vv. 17, 20, 21). After all, it was for his sake that they were being done to death, treated like so many sheep on their way to the slaughter-house (v. 22). Paul was to quote this verse as he looked around at the persecution which he and his fellow-Christians were enduring, as it increased in the early years of the Church's history (Romans 8:36). The psalm ends with a *cri de coeur*—'arise and come to our aid; for your love's sake deliver us' (v. 26).

The psalmist's concern for his people should lead us to pray for the nation of which we are part.

PRAYER

Turn now, O God of hosts;
Behold and tend the vine you have planted.
Keep from trouble all those who trust in you
And forget not the poor for ever.

Have mercy, O Lord, upon us,
As we have put our trust in you.

ROYAL WEDDING

This is another of the royal psalms (see also the comments on Psalms 2, 20 and 72). This, however, is a royal wedding psalm, unique in its form in the Psalter. The plan of the psalm is as follows: A (nameless) writer introduces a song composed in honour of a (nameless) king (v. 1). He addresses the king in flattering terms (vv. 2–9). He addresses the king's bride, his royal consort from Tyre (vv. 10–12). He describes her and her attendants and their arrival at the king's palace with revels and rejoicings (vv. 13–15). He forecasts the result of the union of groom and bride—there will be sons who in due course will be princes. (No mention is made of daughters! We may note their absence also in Psalm 128:3.) Finally, he states his intention to declare the king's fame abroad: 'I shall declare your fame through all generations; therefore nations will praise you for ever and ever' (v. 17).

It is all very colourful and oriental. We hear undertones of national interest—marriage to a Tyrian princess will do much to further international relationships. There is no question about the bride's obeying her husband—he is her lord (v. 11)! But there is more to it than this: *God* has enthroned the king (v. 6). The king may have authority over his people—that is only right. What are kings for, if not for this? *But* he must remember that the ultimate authority over king and people alike is God; that God is concerned with equity, with integrity (v. 6), with right and wrong (v. 7). Only because God sees this in this king has he anointed him 'above his fellows' to this position of authority. God's concern with this monarch is not with his power but with his probity. God's anointed must reflect God's character.

A deeper lesson

At various times of the Church's history, allegory has occupied a major place in the interpretation of the Old Testament. By allegory we mean that the story, or in this case the poem-psalm, is there to give us more than appears on the surface. It is there to hint at—or even to illuminate—a deeper moral or spiritual lesson. To someone using this method of interpretation, the king here described would be Christ himself; his bride would be the Church; his sons would be

Christ's followers in every age. Pressed too hard, the allegorical method can lead—has often led—to ridiculous interpretations.

But in scripture, there is much about the bride relationship of Israel to her God; and Paul delighted in speaking of the Church not only as a building with Christ as its foundation stone, or as the Body of Christ, but also as the Bride (see Ephesians 5:25ff). There is an intimacy in Paul's imagery of the Church as the bride of Christ which goes deeper than that of the building or even of the Body, and has its roots in the Old Testament. For example, the book of the prophet Hosea tells the story of a wife who left her husband for another man. Hosea loved her dearly, and fought to win her back. The tragedy of his broken marriage spoke to Hosea of Israel's desertion of God for idols of wood or stone. He came to see the brokenness of *God's* heart. Thus this 'cross' of Hosea foreshadowed the cross of Christ where the heart of a suffering God is disclosed as nowhere else.

To PONDER

How shall I deal with you, Ephraim?
How shall I deal with you, Judah?
Your loyalty to me is like the morning mist,
like dew that vanishes early.

Hosea 6:4

GOD *our* FORTRESS

Those who lived through the years of World War II may be among the first to appreciate this psalm. It depicts a scene of international chaos—'nations in tumult, kingdoms overturned' (v. 6). The earth was shaking, the waters were seething, the mountains quaking (vv. 2–3). The shape of Europe's map would never be the same again, and now Japan's entry into the war widened the area and deepened the tragedy of world conflict.

Where could people look for help in such time of dire trouble? The writer of this psalm is in no doubt about the answer. '*God* is our refuge and our stronghold' (v. 1). And, lest we forget, he gives us a refrain, in the middle of the psalm and at the end: 'The Lord of hosts is with us; the God of Jacob is our fortress' (vv. 7, 11).

It is an astonishing assurance, coming as it does from little Israel set in the midst of these seething world forces. A city stands where the Most High dwells, a pivotal point of unshakeable serenity (vv. 4–5), the God who delights in breaking bows and snapping spears, the God of peace (v. 9). And this same God reigns, 'exalted among the nations' (v. 10). In him we may have sure confidence, a living hope.

This was doubtless in the mind of Martin Luther (1483–1546) when he wrote:

> *A safe stronghold our God is still,*
> *A trusty shield and weapon;*
> *He'll help us clear from all the ill*
> *That hath us now o'ertaken.*

It is worth our while to read the whole of Luther's hymn, with its defiant confidence. No wonder that it became the rallying cry of the Reformation of the Western Church.

As our psalmist surveys his world, he has in mind his own people, troubled as they are about the chaos which surrounds them. 'Be still,' he writes, 'and know that I am God' (v. 10, Revised Standard Version). 'Let be, then; learn that I am God' (Revised English Bible). 'Pause awhile and know that I am God' (Jerusalem Bible).

A source of comfort

On a more personal level, this psalm has been a source of comfort to many an individual whose world has been shaken and who has been reminded that God is to him or her a 'refuge and a stronghold, a timely help in trouble' (v. 1). The refrain (vv. 7, 11) has assured them and they can see how, in past days, he has wrought astounding deeds (v. 8) for them. They hear God saying to *them*: 'Be still, and know that I am God' (v. 10). The Revised English Bible's rendering of these words is suggestive: 'Let be then; learn that I am God'. *Let be*—'Set your troubled hearts at rest. Trust in God always; trust also in me' (John 14:1).

'Let be then; learn...' Is that a hard lesson to learn? Maybe. But it is imperative that we learn it. 'The style of living in much of current society militates against any inclination to be reflective. Indeed, much of what we are about seems diametrically opposed to the divine command echoed so memorably in Psalm 46: "Be still and know that I am God"'. So wrote Nigel McCulloch, the Bishop of Wakefield, in *The Times* of 2 August, 1997.

When Leslie Weatherhead, the renowned author and preacher, was in charge of a church in Leeds, before he went to Westminster Central Hall, I heard him preach on 'Five Minutes a Day for Health's Sake'. What difference would such a habit bring us if we learned to relax our shoulders—open our hands—fill our lungs, and give God a chance to show us that he is God; if we were open like a ploughed field for the softening of the rain and the warming of the soil? Let be then. Let be. Five minutes a day?

'The adult mind...' wrote Bishop John V. Taylor, 'must be unstriving, receptive, expectant, before there can be any creative insight. Again and again this is the state of mind in which new truth dawns. We do not work it out or think it out; rather, we have the sense of waiting for the disclosure of something that's already there' (*The Go-Between God*, SCM 1972).

MEDITATION

Let be... and learn...

A BROAD CANVAS

The canvas on which this psalmist paints his picture is broad—'all you nations' (v. 1), 'all the earth' (vv. 2, 7), 'God reigns over the nations' (v. 8). There is nothing narrowly nationalistic here. True, God has a special place for the people 'whom he loves', the people of Israel (v. 4), but its God, the awesome Lord Most High, is the 'great King over all the earth' (v. 2). The mighty ones, pagan though they may be, 'belong to God' (v. 9). Such breadth of vision opens the way for the inclusive theology of such a passage as Isaiah 56:1–8, where 'the foreigner who has given his allegiance to the Lord' is welcomed and the eunuch who chooses to do God's will is given a reception better than sons and daughters, and a name in God's own house or within his walls. We can breathe, in an atmosphere such as this!

Crowning the king

This is one of the so-called enthronement psalms (see also Psalm 93 and Psalms 95—99). Sung at the enthronement of a new king, they were probably sung also on the anniversaries of that day. Such celebrations were occasions of great joy and much noisy music. But they were also a reminder that there was a King greater than the one whose day it was, 'the *great* King over all the earth' (v. 7). His dominion was an everlasting one, and to him even a king should bow.

It is appropriate that the Church uses this psalm at Ascensiontide when we think of the exaltation of Christ by 'the King of Glory... with great triumph to your kingdom in heaven.'

In 2 Samuel 6:12–19 the story is told of how David, mindful that God had blessed Obed-Edom's household when he housed the Ark of God, was encouraged to bring it up to the City of David and to set it up in the tent which he had prepared for it. Containing as it did the two stone tablets which had inscribed on them the ten commandments, the Ark spoke supremely of the presence of God himself and his concern for the welfare of his people. The repetition of this drama, on the enthronement of a new king, accompanied by singing and the music of horns, would serve to impress on the people both the awe-ful otherness of God and his nearness to his people. Especially in verses 5–7, one can hear the liturgical overtones of the leader of worship exhorting the people to praise God, and their response to his invitation. Thus:

Leader: *To the shout of triumph God has gone up,*
People: *the Lord has gone up at the sound of the horn.*
Leader: *Praise God, praise him with psalms,*
People: *praise our King, praise him with psalms...*

PRAYER

Grant, O Lord, that both in private prayer
and in the corporate services of the Church,
our hearts may be moved to worship you
and our wills be bent to the gentle rule of your love,
through Jesus Christ our Lord.

The HOLY MOUNTAIN

For many centuries before Christ, the little strip of land which we call Palestine had been one of the most used trade-routes of the world. Through it would pass a stream of camel cavalcades, bearing their treasures from the great nations of Greece and Rome to those as far away as India. When the great temple came to be built on Zion's hill at Jerusalem, the traders must have watched its growth over many years with increasing wonder. So *that* was where Israel's God was supposed to live. 'God shines out from Zion, perfect in beauty' (Psalm 50:2). The writer of Psalm 48 revels in it all—'his holy mountain... fair and lofty, the joy of the whole earth' (v. 2). The temple with its ancillary buildings was a revelation of God as a 'tower of strength' (v. 3).

The effect of all this on visitors from other lands is told with poetic licence and a variety of illustration. Now it is a woman tossing in pain as she awaits the birth of her child (v. 6); now it is a ship threatened with destruction by the force of the wind (v. 7). Here is more than a feat of architecture. Here is a city of the Lord of Hosts, established, never to be shaken: 'What we had heard we saw now with our own eyes in the city of the Lord of Hosts, in the city of our God; God will establish it for evermore' (v. 8). A nation which can produce such a building must be powerful...

God's people at worship

Not only are sightseers from other nations impressed. At verse 9 we move *within* the building where God's people are at worship (v. 9), rejoicing in the God who gives them victory (v. 11). We can see them on their religious processions, marvelling at the number of the towers, the ramparts, the palaces (vv. 12, 13).

Religious buildings, cathedrals and suchlike, vary greatly—and so do those who visit them. Some buildings, alive with the sense of the numinous, speak of God and his beauty. As they kneel to pray, visitors are awestruck as was Jacob in his dream at Harran, and they say: 'How awesome is this place! This is none other than the house of God; it is the gateway to heaven' (Genesis 28:17). Other buildings seem to be not much more than colossal monuments to human megalomania; they elicit no response Godwards. Was our psalmist tempted to see the temple buildings merely as a sign of skill and power on the part of the nation which had produced them? If so, by however small a margin, he avoids that error, for his final word points his readers not to the buildings, but to God himself: 'Such is God, our God for ever; he will be our guide for evermore' (v. 14). He would have empathized with the prophet Zechariah who in his mind's eye saw 'nations and dwellers in many cities' resorting to the Lord of Hosts in Jerusalem, entreating his favour, and saying to their worshipping Jewish friends, 'let us accompany you, for we have heard that God is with you' (Zechariah 8:20–23).

To PONDER

Is the nature of your local church such that people are saying:
'let us accompany you...'?

How does a sightseer (tourist) differ from a person going on
pilgrimage?

Why do you think that Psalm 48 is appointed in some lectionaries
to be used on St Andrew's day (30 November)? You will find a clue
if you link John 1:51 with the story of Jacob's vision mentioned
above (see John 1:40–51).

PSALM 49

FACING *the* FACTS

The man who wrote this psalm sees himself as a prophet. He has a word to speak and he calls on his readers to 'hear', to 'listen' (v. 1), for he himself is a listener (v. 4). I see the opening four verses as a plea to the people to stop talking and start facing the facts of life and death. He plunges into his theme: salvation cannot be bought (vv. 7–9). There is a refrain to this psalm, as if to rub in its lesson: life is short. 'Human beings like oxen are short-lived; they are like beasts whose lives are cut short' (vv. 12, 20). That goes for *all* people: 'the wise die' (v. 10), but the psalmist has a special concern for those whom he calls 'the stupid and senseless' (v. 10), 'the foolish' and their followers (v. 13). These non-listeners, non-thinkers, busy themselves with amassing wealth, building up their estates (vv. 10, 11), giving no thought to the frailty of human existence and the reality of death. He likens them to silly sheep, all following a stupid leader, asking no questions, heading for *Sheol*! They cannot take their money with them nor their estates—all they leave is a name! (vv. 17–18). There is a modern ring to all this...

The ransoming God

It would seem that our psalmist-prophet shares the view expressed in the refrain (vv. 12, 20). *Sheol* is to him a terrible reality (remember our comments on Psalm 6 and elsewhere). The only shaft of light is to be seen in verse 15. He has already stated that 'no man can ever ransom himself' (v. 7). *But* God is the ransoming, rescuing God, able to save him from the power of *Sheol*. Is he referring to life after death? If he is, he gives us in this verse (v. 15) one of the few such instances in the Old Testament, a foretaste of the resurrection hope which is spelled out in its glory in the New Testament. Most scholars, however, do not see it in this way. To them, the power of *Sheol* is the fear of the terror of darkness in this life, a fear from which God can deliver them and will do so in the here and now.

As we saw earlier, the writer who gave us Psalm 8 faces the reality of a mortal's frailty (Psalm 8:4), but he glories in the fact that God himself has 'made him little less than a god, crowning his head with glory and honour'. He is 'master over all that you have made' (Psalm

8:5–6). He reflects the attitude of the writer of the creation story in Genesis 1: 'God created human beings in his own image: in the image of God he created them… and God saw all that he had made, and it was very good' (Genesis 1:27, 31). True, this refers to the situation before the Fall and the need for God's saving 'ransom'. But that we *can* be rescued points to our essential nobility. Even the senseless and the stupid and the foolish—of whom the author of this psalm writes so much—can be stopped from 'heading for *Sheol*' and set on their feet by a redeeming God—if they will hear, if they will listen (Psalm 49:1).

PRAYER

O God… increase and multiply upon us thy mercy; that,
thou being our ruler and guide, we may so pass through things
temporal, that we finally lose not the things eternal: Grant this,
O heavenly Father, for Jesus Christ's sake our Lord.

Collect of Trinity IV, *Book of Common Prayer*

GOD *the* JUDGE

The psalmist paints the picture of a great trial over which God presides as judge. He summons his own people, his 'loyal servants' who live in a covenant relationship with him (vv. 4–5). He shines out from Zion, perfect in its beauty (v. 2), the centre of Jewish worship; but he summons the world from east to west (v. 1), the heavens and the earth (v. 4), to listen to his word which is of universal significance.

After that introduction (vv. 1–6), the rest of the psalm represents the direct speech of God (vv. 7–23). The language is strongly anthropomorphic, attributing human behaviour to God, as we also saw in Psalm 7. The speech is one long protest against ritualism. By that is meant the performance of ritual acts (in this case animal sacrifice) which is unaccompanied by a corresponding insistence on obedience and a godly life on the part of the worshippers. God is not rebuking his hearers for lack of sacrificial offerings—there were plenty of those! He is not hungry (v. 12); he does not eat bull's meat or drink goat's blood! Anyway, he owns all the living creatures of the animal world, including even the birds on the mountains. He is no one's debtor!

Loyalty, not sacrifice

What, then, is the trouble? Not the performance of ritual acts—that may or may not be right. It is the performance of ritual acts divorced from a God-centred life. Put that into New Testament language, and we find it admirably expressed by Jesus himself: 'Not everyone who says to me, 'Lord, Lord', will enter the kingdom of heaven, but only those who do the will of my heavenly Father' (Matthew 7:21). This is a major theme of many of the Old Testament prophets. Hosea puts it starkly: 'I require loyalty, not sacrifice, acknowledgment of God rather than whole-offerings' (Hosea 6:6); and Amos even more pointedly: 'I spurn with loathing your pilgrim-feasts… Spare me the sound of your songs… Instead, let justice flow on like a river and righteousness like a never-failing torrent' (Amos 5:21–24); and Isaiah at greater length: 'Your countless sacrifices, what are they to me?… Wash and be clean… cease to do evil, learn to do good' (Isaiah 1:11–17).

Here in Psalm 50, this theme is searchingly spelled out. God hates alliances made with ungodly people (v. 18), economy with the truth (v. 19), slander (v. 20), forgetfulness of God: 'When you have done these things, and kept silence, you thought that I was someone like yourself; but I shall rebuke you and indict you to your face. You forget God, but think well on this, lest I tear you in pieces and there be no one to save you' (vv. 21–22). *These* are the things that matter, these are the things God hates.

If we may follow the translation of the Revised Standard Version in verse 14, 'make thanksgiving your sacrifice to God', with all that 'thanksgiving' implies of repentance and sincerity, then we can get to the heart of this psalm's message: If our hearts are filled with this true thanksgiving, prayer will be answered, God will come to the rescue of his followers, and he himself will be honoured. And that is 'the chief end of man', as the Scottish catechism puts it.

PRAYER

O God, you desire mercy and not sacrifice,
the knowledge of you rather than burnt offerings:
rule and direct our hearts in the way of true religion
and save us in the day of your appearing:
through Jesus Christ our Lord.

Celebrating Common Prayer

GUILT & JOY

The introductory note to this psalm associates it with the story of David recorded with great detail in 2 Samuel 11. He had committed adultery with Bathsheba, and was responsible for the death of her husband, Uriah. The story ends with the solemn words: 'What David had done was wrong in the eyes of the Lord' (v. 26).

The psalmist is a man labouring under the dark cloud of a guilty conscience. I can hear him say: 'Can God ever forgive me? And can I ever forgive myself?' To think that a sacrificial offering would be of any help is preposterous; God cannot be bought off like that (v. 16)! All the writer can offer is 'a broken spirit... a chastened heart' (v. 17). He comes with empty hands; all he has to offer is the sin for which he needs divine forgiveness. That alone is the offering which God accepts. Given that—a deep repentance (vv. 3, 4)—God can begin his re-creative work and make a new man of him. What he needs is *cardiac* treatment, 'a pure heart' in place of that stained one, a new steadfast spirit in place of that wayward will (v. 10).

That is why this psalm, traditionally sung so often in Anglican churches to a dismal chant, is essentially a psalm of joy. Before we reach its end, we are in the realm of joy (v. 12), praise (v. 15), and the possibility of being of use in God's service: 'I shall teach transgressors your ways, and sinners will return to you' (v. 13). All this is because God delights in creating things, above all, in creating new human beings.

The gift of creativity

When God takes over a human being, he shares with that person his own passion for creating things. That gift of creativity is, I believe, in us all. In many it is allowed to perish, and life as it is meant to be withers. In others it is given free rein and then anything may happen—the musician produces a score, the scholar a book, the artist a picture, the cook a meal, the needleworker a tapestry, the married couple a child. All these people, whether they acknowledge it or not, share in the creative activity of God. In the creation of a *child*, we are at the peak of divine-human creativity—that is why sex is so glorious and sacred a thing.

'Call the world if you please "The Vale of Soul-making",' said the poet John Keats. It is a good phrase. That is what we human beings are here for—to share with the Creator-God the gift of creativity which he has put deep within us, and together—he and I—to produce 'a pure heart... a new and steadfast spirit' (v. 10). An earlier generation spoke and wrote much about 'the soul'. We think more in terms of a noble character, or, best of all, a Christlike character. Paul called it 'sharing the likeness of [God's] Son' (Romans 8:29).

There is hope in this psalm. There is deep penitence for the past; there is forgiveness from the God who can wipe out all iniquity (v. 9). There is delight in the heart of the creator God in the forming of Christ-like character. When he works in me and I work with him, anything may happen. Who said Christianity is dull?

PRAYER

God, create a pure heart for me,
and give me a new and steadfast spirit (v. 10).

50

HUMAN *or* DIVINE RETRIBUTION?

The heading of this psalm associates it with a particular incident in the life of David when the chief of Saul's herdsmen, Doeg, did damage to David by informing against him. The sorry tale can be found in 1 Samuel 21 and 22.

There is some rough stuff here! Clearly, the psalmist has been let down badly, and he is engaging in (enjoying?) pillorying his adversary. That 'mighty man'—can you hear the tone of sarcasm?—has not only brought the writer into disrepute ('infamy') but he brags about doing so (v. 1). He plans his destruction, using his tongue, sharp as a razor to bring that plan into effect (v. 2). He loves falsehood (v. 3), malicious talk and slander (v. 4). What a man to have as your adversary!

It is only natural that the psalmist should turn on him, praying that God will 'fling him to the ground, sweep him away, leave him ruined... uprooted' (v. 5); only natural that he should turn on him, 'laugh at his plight', and mock him (vv. 6, 7).

'Only natural'—yes. But the Christian is called to lead the *super*natural life, to follow in the steps of him who 'when he was abused... did not retaliate, when he suffered... uttered no threats, but delivered himself up to him who judges justly' (1 Peter 2:23). 'My dear friends,' wrote Paul, 'do not seek revenge, but leave a place for divine retribution' (Romans 12:19). So far as we are concerned, it is a matter of 'Hands off. Leave it in God's hands'. Verses 6 and 7 of our psalm do not paint a pretty scene.

A study in contrasts

The closing verses (vv. 8, 9), 'But I am like a spreading olive tree in God's house, for I trust in God's faithful love for ever and ever (v. 8), read in a certain tone, could suggest self-satisfaction, even spiritual pride. Not necessarily, however. The whole psalm—and this is its main use to us—provides us with a study in contrasts—the bragging, 'successful' man of the world (vv. 1–7), over against the man of God (vv. 8, 9). The psalm poses the question: What are our values? Are we mainly concerned with prospering as the majority counts prosperity, of acquiring wealth or status regardless of who gets crushed in the process? Or are we concerned with matters such as trust and love (v. 8), the praise of God and the honour of his name, life among God's loyal servants (v. 9) where, in the fellowship of God's Church, light and growth are to be found?

Suppose this study in contrasts were taken seriously in political life, by the press barons, by the creators of television programmes, by the City magnates, by me—what difference would that make?

PRAYER

Faithful God, full of mercy,
nourish your people in a world of violence;
through prayer and the scriptures
give us the life-giving water of truth
and the rich goodness of your presence;
in Jesus Christ our Lord.

Celebrating Common Prayer

51 PSALM 53 (AND 14)

FINDING GOD

We have caught the psalmist in a despondent mood. Did he get out of bed the wrong side on the morning he wrote this psalm? 'What's wrong with the human race?' he keeps saying. 'No one does good, no, not even one' (v. 3). He paints a grim picture.

He pinpoints the error of those impious fools, as he calls them. They say: 'There is no God.' That does not mean that they are all atheists—that is far too modern a word to use. If we asked anyone living in the age of the psalmists whether he believed in God, he would reply: 'Yes, of course.' His world was full of gods; to one or more of them he gave allegiance, though it was an allegiance often tinged with terror at the unpredictable use of power on the part of that god or those gods. The trouble with the psalmist's 'impious fool' was not that he denied the *existence* of God—he took that for granted. The trouble was that he denied God's *activity*. God seemed to him to be absent from the world where monstrous atrocities were happening. The fool could devour others as people devour food—and get away with it. The day would come when God's judgment would be seen: of that the psalmist was assured (v. 5). But that conviction was far from the thoughts of the fool.

Radical wrongness

Was the gloom of our writer merely the result of a bad night? Or was he putting his finger on a fact we often fail to face, namely, the reality of the radical wrongness which marks and mars the race of which we are a part? The theologians call it original sin; but that phrase has been so misunderstood that, at least for a while, we had best avoid it. Perhaps it would be more helpful if we began by recognizing human beings as the crown of the created order as we now see it. So far as we know, we alone have the ability to *respond* to God. Human greatness consists in that response. Human misery derives from our refusal to respond.

God is at the centre of all life. We are ec-centric (out of centre) in so far as we deny that, or fail to live by its implications. On the cosmic scale, we see this principle at work when we consider what ensues when we defile earth, rivers or seas by spewing poisons into them. On the personal scale we see what happens to our lungs and hearts when we smoke, to our hearts and livers when we over-eat or over-drink, or to our characters when we maintain wrong relationships with our fellows.

The old picture-story of Adam and Eve, the fruit and the snake, makes uncomfortable reading to those who have been accustomed to think of the human race as being on the up and up in the evolutionary process. The schoolboy, asked to translate the *status quo* did so in the immortal words: 'The mess we're in'. Was he far out? Or was our psalmist? Those who want to pursue this subject might profit by reading Geoffrey Paul's *A Pattern of Faith* and especially the chapter 'God's World, or Whose?'

To PONDER

God created human beings in his own image;
in the image of God he created them;
male and female he created them.

Genesis 1:27

No one does good, no, not even one.

Psalm 53:3

52

PEACE *in the* STORM

In the Introduction we referred to the constant use throughout the Psalter of parallelism. In this psalm we have good examples of it.

In verse 1, the first line 'Save me, O God, by the power of your name', is paralleled by 'and vindicate me through your might'. In verse 2, the first line 'God, hear my prayer', is paralleled by 'listen to my supplication'. Verse 3 is another example.

Parallelism is a useful device. Often the second line adds no new idea to the first. It simply serves to underline it, to emphasize it. It corresponds to our use of italics. At other times, the second line introduces a new element which registers the point of the first line and adds a fresh touch of meaning to it. The reader of the psalms does well to look out for parallelism—its presence, and its effect.

If we search our hearts, we can probably recall moments in our own experience when we have come close to sympathy with the psalmist's attitude in verse 5 and in the second line of verse 7. We would, of course, put it more politely than the psalmist did... ! It is a natural reaction when one is hurt. But the Christian attitude is *super*natural. 'Love your enemies and pray for your persecutors' (Matthew 5:44). See also the note on imprecatory psalms in the Introduction.

The introductory note to this psalm associates it with the story recorded in 1 Samuel 23, where David is being chased from pillar to post under intense pressure from the Philistines. One can overhear the intensity of desire as he turns to God: 'Save me... vindicate me... hear my prayer...'. The storm is raging. Life is cheap, and who knows what may happen? But there are signs of the triumph of faith: 'God is my helper, the Lord the sustainer of my life...' (v. 4), and even a bold declaration of the future regarded as a fact already experienced: 'God *has* rescued me...' (v. 7). There is peace at the heart of the storm.

Trust in God always

In John's description of the events leading up to the crucifixion of Jesus, he tells of Judas' exit from supper to betray his Master, of Peter's bragging, of the bewilderment of the other ten apostles (John

13:21–38). Then, immediately: 'Set your troubled hearts at rest,' says Jesus. 'Trust in God always; trust also in me' (John 14:1). 'Let not your hearts be storm-tossed' (the verb can be used of heaving seas). Mark, in his story of the squall on the lake of Galilee, describes the terrified disciples and Jesus at peace in the midst of it all. At his word, the storm subsides (Mark 4:35–41).

'Peace is my parting gift to you, my own peace, such as the world cannot give. Set your troubled hearts at rest, and banish your fears' (John 14:27). 'My parting gift'—it's a lovely legacy.

PRAYER

May the peace of God, which is beyond all understanding, guard
our hearts and our thoughts in Christ Jesus.

BETRAYAL

There are not many other psalms in which the writer spells out his misery in more detail than this one. Panic, anguish, the terrors of death, fear and trembling—his language is almost exhausted. And the description of his torturers is almost as detailed. But the most unusual feature is the directness with which one man is singled out. We seem only to lack his name (vv. 12–14; vv. 20–21). We can see the psalmist point his finger at him. We can hear his voice, rising to a shriek—'It was you... a comrade, my own dear friend'. That they used to hold pleasant converse together, 'walking with the throng in the house of God', only made things worse.

This corresponds to real experience. It is one thing to be faced with opposition, even with a flood of it. It is quite another to be betrayed by a friend. In that, there is heartache beyond description.

On verses 9, 15 and 23 see my comments on verses 5 and 7 of Psalm 54.

The wings of a dove

No wonder, then, that the poet longs to get away from it all—'Oh that I had the wings of a dove to fly away... !' (v. 6). In the 1930s, a choirboy, Ernest Lough, sang Mendelssohn's 'Hear my Prayer'. Recordings have made his rendering known the world over. Even today they breathe the peace for which our psalmist yearned. The prayer is perfectly natural. We do not know whether it was answered in the affirmative or not. Sometimes God does so respond: he provides a way of escape. But often it is answered by a firm and loving 'No; no escape route this time, my child. Not "away from it all", but *through* it all *with me*. In my company you shall learn lessons which will strengthen you in a way that escape never would. We will go through it together. You will be a stronger character in the end.'

Three times a day the psalmist made his prayer (v. 17). Was God a little hard of hearing? Did he need reminding? There is something to be said for being importunate! We do not know how it all turned out. But his exhortation to his readers to 'commit your fortunes to the Lord, and he will sustain you' (freed from his obvious desire for retribution on his enemies) is one to make our own (v. 22). He has been a burdened and an embittered man. He bids us 'unload your burden on to Yahweh' (Jerusalem Bible). He reminds us of Peter's injunction: 'He cares for you, so cast all your anxiety on him' (1 Peter 5:7). I hope he found peace in the end.

MEDITATION

We all get wounded. We all at times want to 'fly away and find rest'. Sometimes God has a better way for us. Paul speaks of two kinds of pain and two ways of bearing it: 'pain borne in God's way' and 'pain borne in the world's way' (2 Corinthians 7:10). The results are very different. The first results in 'a change of heart leading to salvation', a fuller life, greater wholeness. The other results in death. On the word 'death', Paul does not comment. No comment is called for.

An EMPHASIS *on* GOD

One feature marks this psalm. It is its constant emphasis on *God*. We run our eye down over the verses, and the emphasis stands out— 'I put my trust in you, the Most High... in God... in God... in the Lord...' The writer elaborates the difficulties which he has to face, and they are many and deeply hurtful. He does not deny the reality of the evil which has hit him. But by his constant turning to God he avoids the peril of sinking into a morass of self-pity. He seeks to rise above it into the pure air of God's presence. He stays himself on the fact that God does notice—the psalmist's grief and tears are recorded by God (v. 8). (For another reference to God's book, we may note Moses' conviction that his name is written in it (Exodus 32:32). A similar concept is found in Malachi 3:16—'a record was written before [God] of those who feared him and had respect for his name'.

To heed this emphasis on God is to be delivered from an introspective religiosity. (Cast your eye down the Index of First Lines of your favourite hymnbook, and see how many of the hymns begin with 'I'!) A guide to the development of our spiritual life might well be: 'For every look within take ten looks up to God.'

Walking in the light

To *walk* in the presence of God (v. 13) is to go about our daily life, to conduct ourselves in the light which God provides. The spiritual life as a walk is a favourite concept in Scripture. We should recall that there was no street lighting in biblical times. We grumble about treacherous paving in our streets, and we see elderly people, a stick in one hand and a torch in the other, seeking to avoid a fall. What must it have been like when there were no lights at all! Temptations are subtle and assault us through life, to the end. One can easily slip and spoil the development of a strong Christian character. There is no need, if we 'walk in the presence of God, in the light of life'. Poet and theologian John Henry Newman (1801–90) rightly prayed:

Keep thou my feet; I do not ask to see
the distant scene; one step enough for me.

And then, with a confidence which he shared with our psalmist, he asserted:

So long thy power hath blessed me, sure it still
will lead me on...

And the Hebridean crofters prayed as they went to their work:

With God be my walking this day,
with Christ be my walking this day,
with Spirit my walking this day,
the Threefold all-kindly my way:
Ho, ho, ho! The Threefold all kindly I pray.

MEDITATION

What kind of inscription would you like on your gravestone? '[S]he walked in the presence of God, in the light of life'—how would that do? It is much to be coveted.

The WRITER & HIS GOD

No one could accuse our psalmist of being colourless in his use of language. He is not meticulous to avoid mixing his metaphors; man-eating lions 'whose teeth are spears and arrows, whose tongues are sharp swords'—that's quite a picture!

The main interest in this psalm consists in the relationship between the writer and his God, and his concern for God's honour and glory. We see the latter in the refrain of verses 5 and 11: 'God, be exalted above the heavens; let your glory be over all the earth'.

His relationship with God is described in the opening verse. God is his refuge, in the shadow of whose wings he can find shelter 'until the storms are past'. In this picture I see the new-born bird nestling close to the mother-bird, safe under her wings while the wind howls and the rain splashes down. People have mocked the Christian faith as being a crutch for the feeble. Let us admit the charge. Society is full of feeble people, the most feeble being those who boast their own strength most loudly! There are hosts of people wounded and crippled by 'the slings and arrows of outrageous fortune' (*Hamlet*, Act 3 Scene 1). Life for them is full of hurts—and they need a crutch; and they find it in him who bore our sins and carried our sorrows. Thank God for that.

But, of course, the Christian faith is far, far more than a crutch for the feeble. The wise men of Judaism knew that, long before the Christian faith was born, and our psalmist was one of them. If verse 1 is an admission of human frailty, verse 3 gives us the confidence of a man who knows where to find 'salvation'; God 'will send from heaven and save me', the God whose love is 'unfailing and sure'.

The secret of salvation

The range of the psalmist's thought is impressive. He has found the secret of salvation (life to the full) in God, and he is concerned to praise him 'among the peoples... among the nations' (v. 9)—no narrow horizons for him! As he looks at the nations beyond the borders of Israel, he sees their pathetic gods of wood and stone and longs that their worshippers should know the never-failing faithfulness of the God of Abraham, Isaac and Jacob—*his* God. A church which has no missionary passion is likely to die soon.

As for the psalmist himself, there is to be no lying abed for him! He addresses himself: 'Awake, my soul'. He will be up at dawn and at his prayers and praises (v. 8). Discipleship implies discipline.

Thomas Ken, Bishop of Bath and Wells, was surely meditating on this psalm when he wrote one of his best-known hymns. And we can share his thoughts:

MEDITATION

Awake, my soul, and with the sun
Thy daily stage of duty run;
Shake off dull sloth, and joyful rise
To pay thy morning sacrifice.

Wake, and lift up thyself, my heart,
And with the angels bear thy part,
Who all night long unwearied sing
High praises to the eternal King.

Bishop Thomas Ken (1637–1710)

POWERFUL LANGUAGE

There are those who would write off this poem as a nasty piece of work. 'Look at the language used in verses 3 to 10,' they would say. 'Even the comment on imprecatory psalms in the Introduction hardly covers *this* psalm!'

Before we agree too readily with this judgment we must note that:

- firstly, no names are mentioned. There is no threat to any specific person. It is 'you rulers' who are addressed (v. 1).

- secondly, the poet is assuming the role of a prophet, in the biblical sense of that word. That is to say, he is not primarily concerned with forecasting the future. He is concerned with receiving a word from God and conveying it to those who will listen. In this case, it is about God as a God of justice, who is revolted by the actions of responsible people who could not care less about inhumanity to their fellows. They regard neither humanity nor God.

Martyr-prophets

The opening two verses of this psalm could have served, word for word, as a text for Mahatma Gandhi in his leadership of civil disobedience for India's oppressed people; and for Martin Luther King in his campaign against the segregation of Black people in America; and for Dietrich Bonhoeffer in his opposition to the Nazi regime; and for Nelson Mandela in his fight against apartheid in South Africa; and for Archbishop Oscar Romero of El Salvador in his plea for thousands of his fellow-countrymen who 'disappeared' and were never seen again. We could go on with illustrations even in our own lifetime, not to mention atrocities which have blackened the history-books of ages gone by. Was the language of these martyr-prophets always polite? God is mocked and society is shamed while these iniquities persist. Obsequious language will not avail. Disgusting policies, twisted law-court judgments, call forth disgusting language—sometimes its use is the only way by which consciences can be pricked and repentance translated into action.

This psalm would say to the rulers and the judges, 'There is, after all, a God who dispenses justice on earth (v. 11), even if you do not.

Your fate is sealed.' Perhaps it would arouse a blush on *our* cheeks if we recall that we did not protest when a Jewish person was excluded from membership of our club, or a black or disabled person or a woman from inclusion on a shortlist for a job?

PRAYER

From moral weakness of spirit, from timidity, from hesitation, from fear of men and dread of responsibility, strengthen us to speak the truth… with the strength that can yet speak in love and self-control; and alike from the weakness of hasty violence and the weakness of moral cowardice, save us and help us, we humbly beseech thee, O Lord.

From Bishop George Ridding, *A Litany of Remembrance*

57

A WOUNDED MAN

What a strange psalm this is! It reminds me of a spring day, when periods of storm alternate with periods of sunshine. Now the clouds threaten and down comes the rain; now the sun comes out with welcome warmth and the promise of spring and summer is in the air. So our psalmist writes, describing in nasty detail his opponents, and then giving us a picture of his gracious God. This is then repeated in a kind of series of layers.

His opponents are described in more personal detail than were the opponents of the man who wrote Psalm 58. Our psalmist has been verbally abused—he is a wounded man (v. 7)—and the dogs are snarling at him (note the repetition in verses 6 and 14); we can hear their howling as the mongrels disturb the peace of the night. The writer hopes that God will pay them out—they deserve it!

Shafts of sunshine

That is the stormy side of the psalmist's experience. But in between the lines which describe these bloodthirsty men come shafts of sunshine as he describes the God whom he wants to worship (v. 17) but who, it would seem, needs to be roused and woken up (v. 5). We may well dislike his desire for revenge (v. 11), but his descriptions of his God are well worth our considering:

- God is a *tower* (vv. 1, 9, 16). When a town was surrounded by enemy forces and about to be sacked, the last stages of resistance usually found the citizens sheltering in a strongly fortified tower.

- He is *Israel's God*, the God who down the centuries has proved himself in the history of his people. He is the Lord God of Hosts (v. 5). He is a shield (v. 11), a refuge in the day of trouble (v. 16). He is the writer's strength (vv. 9, 16, 17). He is—best of all—'my gracious God' (v. 17). Grace is love in action.

As we read this strangely mixed psalm, we register dislike of the writer's desire to gloat over his enemies' downfall (v. 10) and the traces of smugness which mark his self-description (vv. 3, 4). But we see at the same time a man struggling to keep his hold on God, experiencing much of the strength and grace of God who keeps hold on *him*, and determined to raise a psalm of praise to God his strength, his strong tower, his gracious God (v. 17).

A tangled character indeed. But aren't we all?

PRAYER

O ingenious God,
I rejoice in your creation,
and pray that your Spirit touch me so deeply
that I will find a sense of self
which makes me glad to be who I am
and yet restless
at being anything less
than I can become.

From Ted Loder, *Guerillas of Grace*

NATIONAL DEFEAT

The character of the man who wrote this psalm stands out clearly. He loves the nation of which he is a member and cares deeply about his fellow-citizens. He shares their shame in whatever national humiliation has come to them. They have suffered such a defeat as to leave them dizzy. He can only think that God in his anger has been behind it. That much is clear from the opening three verses. However, the situation is not past redemption (v. 4). The writer turns to prayer: 'Save with your right hand and respond, that those dear to you may be delivered' (v. 5).

God is not silent. He speaks from his sanctuary—and we note the inverted commas of verses 6 to 8. The Hebrew text is difficult and may have become corrupt as it was copied and handed down over long years. But these verses depict God as a man of war, using Ephraim (the northern kingdom of Israel) as his helmet and Judah as his sceptre (v. 7; a royal touch here).

As for Moab and Edom and Philistia, those wretched countries which were always snapping at Israel's heels, language can hardly be found sufficiently degrading to describe them (v. 8)! *Moab* is merely God's washbowl, and as for *Edom*—to cast your shoe at someone is to insult him beyond limit. The scholar Dr Kenneth E. Bailey has written an illuminating book about the peoples of the ancient Near East (*Past and Present Through Peasant Eyes*). He shows that 'to cast a shoe' is to engage in a very strong insult—it once caused a riot of 1,000 students!

A bitter cry

'That's all very well', the psalmist seems to say. 'But, God, whom will you *use* to do what you have promised—to blast his way into the fortified city and reduce the miserable Edomites once and for all? It would seem that you have rejected us and abdicated from your military leadership' (v. 10). It is a bitter cry. In verse 8, *Philistia* is called to acclaim God. (In the almost identical passage in Psalm 108:9, the text reads 'I shout my war-cry against Philistia'.) At verse 8 the divine speech ends. God is not a mere spectator when his people are crushed, as verses 1–3 and 10 might suggest!

But hope, even though it is very frail, triumphs over despair. Mere human effort will not avail. God himself *will* act… (vv. 11–12). The psalmist falls to prayer. Hope is not dead.

PRAYER

You are my hope, Lord God,
my trust since my childhood.

Psalm 71:5

Our Father,
give us each day a steady faith,
an expectant hope,
an outgoing love,
through Jesus Christ our Lord.

ENDS *of the* EARTH

The opening two verses of this psalm strike a note of deep pathos. The writer cries to God 'from the end of the earth'. We can take this literally: far from the land of Judea, the homesick exile cries to God. Or we can take it metaphorically: like the writer of Psalm 130:1 who cried 'out of the depths', this writer feels distanced from his God. Can God hear? Will he do so? The psalmist is depressed—'Lift me up,' he cries. Some people in such a plight would give up praying. Not he; as he prays, his confidence grows, and he dares, like the writer of Psalm 59, to speak of God in terms like 'rock', and 'shelter' and 'tower of strength' (vv. 2, 3). It was Jesus himself who told his followers a parable 'to show that they should keep on praying and never lose heart' (Luke 18:1).

'The cover of your wings'. We met a similar phrase in Psalm 57:1 and thought of the mother-bird and her chicks. It is a thought worth pursuing. But there is more to the phrase than that. The Ark, the sacred symbol of God's presence, had two gold cherubim 'with wings spread out and pointing upwards' (Exodus 25:20). To be in God's 'tent' (v. 4)—memories of the wilderness wanderings were never far from the psalmist's mind—was to be near those sheltering wings, awesome yet welcoming (for other uses of this illustration, see 17:8; 36:7; 57:1). And even when the Ark had a more permanent resting place, in the temple building itself, the temple was still referred to as God's 'tent'.

God's promise

Verses 6–7, calling for God's blessing on the king, are strangely interruptive. Omit them, and verse 8 runs on logically from verse 5. Many people think that they have slipped in here accidentally, in the long process of copying and re-copying the psalms and handing them down to successive generations of readers. That may well be the case. However, the wording of verses 6 and 7 recalls the promise of God to King David and given by Nathan to the king: 'Your family and your kingdom will be established for ever in my sight; your throne will endure for all time' (2 Samuel 7:16). The king in his own person is one with his people. If he stands under God's protection, 'abiding in

God's presence' and preserved by God's 'true and constant love' (v. 7), his welfare will include that of his people. There is *communion* of king and subjects under the immortal and invisible King.

In our first paragraph, we thought of people who were at 'the end of the earth', or in 'the depths' of despair. We speak of such people as having 'reached the end of their tether', distressed to the limit of their endurance. The writer of the next psalm has some advice which, if taken, will surprise those who have never shared their grief with God: 'Trust in him at all times, you people; pour out your hearts before him; God is our shelter' (Psalm 62:8). They may even learn to sing again (v. 8).

PRAYER

I love you, O Lord, you alone,
my refuge on whom I depend;
my maker, my saviour, my own,
my hope and my trust without end;
the Lord is my strength and my song,
defender and guide of my ways;
my master to whom I belong,
my God who shall have all my praise.

Christopher Idle

60 PSALM 62

HOLLOW LIVES

Against a sinister background of people who threaten him and aim to topple him (vv. 3, 4), the psalmist gives us a statement about the basis of his life with God—'he alone is my rock of deliverance...' (v. 6). We note the refrain of verses 1 and 2 with verses 5 and 6. The theme of waiting silently for God reminds us of Psalm 40.

Some people have detected a touch of self-satisfaction, of superiority, in this psalm: 'I'm all right, Jack. You're all wrong.' I do not read it this way. The writer is a realist. He looks around on his fellow citizens and is impressed with the sheer emptiness of the life they lead. They have no moral standards. There is no weight to them. They are given over to the trivial, the passing, the material. Mammon matters above all else. It is all so hollow (vv. 9, 10).

He cannot go with them in this shallow way of living. Surely there is more to life than that! Is it possible to maintain a vigorous spiritual life with this dark fog around him? 'For God alone I wait silently; my deliverance comes from him'—given that, he will remain unshaken (v. 6).

A clear witness

His witness is clear. In waiting silently, he learned two things—the power of God, and the unfailing love of God. Indeed there are three things—he learned of the justice of the God who rewards 'everyone according to what he has done' (vv. 11, 12). That is the foundation of his life. And he can at all times rely on the faithfulness of God.

Nor can he keep this confidence to himself. He turns to the people and addresses them: 'Trust in him... pour out your hearts before him' (v. 8); 'do not set your heart on' wealth, still less on extortion and robbery (v. 10). The writer has learned the lesson that when you have found a good thing you share it. If you don't you will lose it.

MEDITATION—& ACTION

How do I know that God is good? I don't.
I gamble like a man. I bet my life
Upon one side in life's great war. I must,
I can't stand out. I must take sides. The man
Who is neutral in the fight is not
A man. He's bulk and body without breath,
Cold leg of lamb without mint sauce. A fool.
He makes me sick. Good Lord! Weak tea! Cold slops!
I want to live, live out, not wobble through
My life somehow, and then into the dark.
I must have God. This life's too dull without,
Too dull for aught but suicide.

Geoffrey A. Studdert-Kennedy (1883–1929)

61

THIRSTING *for* GOD

Apart from the fierce verses of 9 and 10, there is a strong element of
serenity about this psalm. The psalmist writes of his thirst and his
longing for God, and it is clear that, at least partially, that thirst has
been satisfied. Jesus, we recall, said that those who so hungered and
thirsted would indeed be satisfied (Matthew 5:6).

The dry land, parched and devoid of water (v. 1), is a vivid
metaphor. We who live in gentle climates are largely unfamiliar with
what drought and a blazing sun can do to a field—until David
Attenborough in some nature film on television shows us. Great
cracks break open in the soil and cry out for rain. Then it comes in
torrents—and almost at once (or so it seems) the cracks are washed
away and the green shoots appear.

It was so with this writer. He knew he was made for God, and he
longed for him—longed for him in the temple when he worshipped
with God's people (v. 2); called him to mind when he lay on his bed
(v. 6; see also Psalms 3:5 and 4:8). In the sanctuary he saw something of the power and glory of God (v. 2); on his bed he experienced
something of the nearness of God, under the shadow of his wings,
upheld by his right hand (vv. 7, 8). 'My soul clings close to you, your
right hand supports me' (v. 8, Jerusalem Bible)—there is the intimacy
of a divine-human embrace in that verse. He has found something
better than life itself (v. 3). No wonder he bursts out into praise of
God (vv. 3–5): 'Your unfailing love is better than life; therefore I shall
sing your praises' (v. 3). No wonder he is serene. In that praise and
in that serenity of confidence, king and commoner can join (v. 11).

Rest and calm

I once wrote an article on 'Shoulders that Speak'. In it I suggested that
often you can tell a great deal about someone's character by the way
he holds himself. If his shoulders are hunched and his muscles taut,
it indicates a man ill at ease. If his shoulders are relaxed, his muscles
loose, it intimates a measure of rest and calm. I ended the article with
these words: 'Would it not be true to say that the world's greatest
need is an infusion of Christian women and men who are strong

enough in God, obedient enough to God, to breathe into the world's hectic hassle something of his peace, and through their silent waiting on God share something of his passion for the world's salvation?'

'God, you are my God; I seek you eagerly with a heart that thirsts for you...' (v. 1). The 'satisfaction' which Jesus promised (Matthew 5:6) does not generally come with a rush. It comes as we daily learn to wait on God.

MEDITATION

I smiled to think God's greatness flowed round our incompleteness;
Round our restlessness his rest.

Elizabeth Barrett Browning (1806–61)

TRUE LAMENT

It is good, sometimes, to get things off your chest in the presence of God. Certainly the psalmist did so. He describes his particular 'thing' in considerable detail. Without seeming to be unsympathetic, we could have done with a shorter list! Terror, intrigues, a mob of evil-doers with sharp tongues shooting down innocent people, hiding their snares, hatching their plots—he does go on—six full verses of it! This psalm is 'a lament' all right. As I read it I begin to wonder whether the writer was not multiplying his troubles simply by dwelling so long on them, the mere repetition exacerbating the problem.

We have all met people like this—or perhaps even *been* people like this. The list of their physical complaints is so long and so detailed that we sometimes wondered (in our wickedness) whether they did not rather enjoy ill-health. The hypochondriac is not the best of companions at any time; the air gets thick with his complaints.

A shaft of light

Have I been too hard on the writer? Perhaps so. A shaft of light lifts the gloom even if only momentarily. Unlike his tormentors who mutter 'who will see us?' as they hide their snares (v. 5), he does not leave God out of the picture. He addresses God (v. 1); he believes in the activity of God—he has an arsenal with which to shoot bows at them (with verses 3 and 4 compare verse 7); God will be the source of his joy and refuge (v. 10). There are signs that the psalmist knows how to open the windows and let the fresh air and sunshine in.

We can find a similar demonstration of trust in God in Isaiah 12, a little psalm standing on its own. Its second verse runs: 'God is my deliverer. I am confident and unafraid'. In the Authorized Version it runs: 'Behold, God is my salvation; I will trust, and not be afraid'. It enshrines a great lesson. The hymn writer Bishop Walsham How was referring to his sins when he wrote the lines:

At thy feet I lay them,
And I leave them there.

But, surely, we may use these words of our ills and misfortunes, whether they come at us from outside (as the psalmist thought his did) or from within, perhaps because of our self-centredness. Could we add another beatitude to the list given in Matthew 5: 'Blessed are the window-openers'? For good reason, the third Person of the blessed Trinity is spoken of in scripture in terms of *wind*. He is the Lord. He is the Life-giver. He refreshes. He renews. He reinvigorates.

PRAYER *to the* HOLY SPIRIT

Heal our wounds; our strength renew;
On our dryness pour thy dew;
Wash the stains of guilt away;
Bend the stubborn heart and will;
Melt the frozen, warm the chill;
Guide the steps that go astray.

Archbishop Stephen Langton (c. 1160–1228)
and Edward Caswall (1814–78)

WORSHIP *at the* TEMPLE

Psalm 65 is as light-hearted as Psalm 64 was heavy-hearted. There is only one touch of sadness in it (v. 3a), and that is relieved by the possibility of forgiveness (v. 3b). Even the valleys, decked with grain, join the psalmist in his song of praise (v. 13).

In verses 4 and 5 we join God's people in the corporate worship of the temple—we linger in the courts of God, in his house. We find ourselves with many from beyond the bounds of Israel; more and more foreigners, intelligent and dissatisfied with their own religions with their many gods and goddesses, were being drawn towards the ethical teaching of the God of the Jewish law-givers and prophets.

From the temple, our thoughts move out to the mountains and seas of the created order (vv. 6–8). The impact of the mountains and the calming of the raging seas speak of the power of almighty God. Even the pagans are overawed by it.

The beauty of the earth

From the vastness of creation, we move to the wonder of Mother Earth, for which God himself has a care and concern. Verses 9 to 13 are surely one of the most picturesque passages in the Bible. The writer knew his countryside and loved it with something of its Creator's love: 'You crown the year with your good gifts; places where you have passed drip with plenty' (v. 11). One greater than the psalmist was to illustrate his teaching again and again by the use of nature parables; Jesus himself was a country man.

Soil is sacred stuff. I believe that much of present-day crime is due to the fact that those who live in the sprawl of the great cities across the world are divorced from the countryside. To be close to the soil is to be close to sanity. To inhale the air of the country makes a healthier—dare we even say holier—person than one who lives in an atmosphere polluted by petrol fumes or tobacco smoke.

There is a note of sheer delight in the last five verses of this psalm. What would its author have said (or sung) if he had been able to enjoy the fruits of colour photography; or to view the nature films which feature on our television screens; or to stand and stare at Van Gogh's *Sunflowers*, or his *Meadow with Cypress Trees*, or even his

Cornfield with Crows? We are so much richer than he—but are we more thankful? For him the naked but observant eye and the thankful worshipping heart were enough to open his lips in praise—'it is *fitting* to praise you in Zion, God' (v. 1). After all, he was doing his share in appreciating the earth which God so dearly loves.

Let us PRAISE

To thee, O Lord, our hearts we raise
In hymns of adoration,
To thee bring sacrifice of praise
With shouts of exultation.
Bright robes of gold the fields adorn,
The hills with joy are ringing,
The valleys stand so thick with corn
That even they are singing.

William Chatterton Dix (1837–98)

BLESSING GOD

This is essentially a psalm of *worship*. It begins with a summons to all the earth to acclaim God and sing to the glory of his name (vv. 1–4). It ends with the psalmist blessing the God who has blessed him (v. 20).

We could call verses 5 to 7 'the approach to history'. Constantly the Old Testament writers looked back, and bade their readers look back, to God's interventions on behalf of his people Israel. The supreme example and the one most repeatedly quoted was that of the Exodus. Here, in the emergence of the nation from Egyptian tyranny and in its eventual entry into the promised land, they saw God's hand at work (Exodus 3ff). He had 'bared his arm'—we might say 'had muscled in' for them. He had established a covenant relationship with them. Hence the summons of this psalm to praise.

A refining process

Not that the Israelites had had it easy all the way. It had been no path of roses. Their very lives had been in peril, their feet in danger of stumbling (v. 9). Sometimes as a result of their own folly and way-wardness, sometimes as a result of circumstances beyond their control, they had gone through fire and water (v. 12), they had been entrapped (v. 11). It had been a refining process (v. 10). Yes; a *refining* process. Silver can only be seen at its shining best when it has been through the fire. People often find God at that painful point. It was in the midst of the fire that the three young men in Daniel's story found one who looked 'like a god' (Daniel 3:25).

This, the psalmist would say, was true for the nation of Israel. This, he would say, was true for him. A principle was at work. God was at work. 'Say to God, "how awesome are your deeds!"' (v. 3).

Out of a full heart he found himself asking what he could give to God in return for his goodness (vv. 13–15). He answered in terms of the things by which his own fortune, big or small, had been acquired: rams and bulls and goats. His modern opposite number would speak in terms of cash and material possessions. He must give of his best. He must? No. Gratitude made him give with delight. 'God loves a *cheerful* giver,' Paul said. The word translated 'cheerful' is in Greek *hilaros*—with all that that suggests of fun and even of abandon. Hilarious giving—that's quite a thought! (2 Corinthians 9:7).

INVITATION

Come and see what God has done (v. 5).
Come, listen… and I shall tell you what he has done for me (v. 16).

RESPONSE

Blessed be God who has not withdrawn from me his love and care.

REMEMBERING GOD'S PURPOSES

This is one of the most familiar of the psalms. In the 1662 version of the *Book of Common Prayer*, it was appointed as the alternative to the *Nunc Dimittis* in the service of Evening Prayer. It opens with a prayer which all of us would want to pray. We need God's smile if we are to be happy, so may he 'be gracious to us and bless us, may he cause his face to shine on us' (v. 1). It is based on the blessing of Aaron: 'May the Lord bless you and guard you; may the Lord make his face shine on you and be gracious to you; may the Lord look kindly on you and give you peace' (Numbers 6:24–26).

It could, of course, be a selfish prayer—God bless *me*! Some Christians have scarcely got beyond A.A. Milne's poem of the little boy, saying, 'God bless Mummy' and *just* remembering to ask him to bless Daddy as well!

> *God bless Mummy. I know that's right.*
> *Wasn't it fun in the bath tonight?*
> *The cold's so cold, and the hot's so hot.*
> *Oh! God bless Daddy—I quite forgot.*

Nothing could be further from the psalmist's mind. Why does he pray this prayer? He prays it in order that God's 'purpose may be known on earth' (v. 2 and note the similar thought in v. 7). The earth is the Lord's, as we saw in Psalm 24:1. He made it. He cares about it. He put humans in it to act as his agents (see the opening chapters of Genesis). He has a purpose for it—he would not have it relapse into chaos. And he wants all the people in it to know his 'saving power' (v. 2b), his plan that the earth's inhabitants should live their lives to the full as children of the Most High.

In fact, Psalm 67 is one of the most unselfish psalms in the book. The writer's concern is for 'all nations' (v. 2), 'all peoples' (v. 3), 'nations, peoples, nations' (v. 4), 'all the peoples' (v. 5), 'the ends of the earth' (v. 7). He shares God's love for the *world*.

Wider horizons

Perhaps it is understandable that one of the most besetting sins of the British people is our insularity. Shakespeare gloried in

> *This precious stone set in the silver sea,*
> *Which serves it in the office of a wall,*
> *Or as a moat defensive to a house*
> *Against the envy of less happier lands...* (Richard II Act 2 Scene 1)

That was truer in his day than in ours, for the Channel Tunnel has linked us to Europe and air travel to the world. We are less of an island than we were. But the insularity of *mind* persists. Nor is the church exempt from it. If you doubt this, consider two things:

- One of the tests of the spiritual health of a church (diocese, parish) is its record of sending its members on overseas errands. One of the richest dioceses of the Anglican Communion gives large sums every year to the church at home and to charitable causes. It has so many clergy that it has difficulty in placing them in its parishes. But in sending men and women to work for God further afield, its record is shameful. It is easier to send money than men and women. *That* is truly costly.

- In the ministry of intercession, how wide is our range? How personal is our interest? How intimate is our concern? We constantly need to enlarge the horizons of our prayer beyond our own domestic and local concerns to embrace the whole world, as the psalmist did.

MEDITATION

God so loved the world.

John 3:16

Christ loved the church, and gave himself up for it.

Ephesians 5:25

The Christian's love must be no narrower than that.

GOD'S TENDER CARE

This psalm is similar to Psalm 66 in that its author looks back to history and from that backward look derives his lessons for the present and the future. Various incidents from Israel's story are poetically described and are made the basis for a call to worship and praise God (vv. 4–6; 32–35). There are parallels between this psalm and the great poem of Judges 5 sung by Deborah and Barak after the Israelites' victory over the Canaanites.

The theme is set out in the opening verses. What is more ephemeral than a puff of smoke driven by the wind, or what is more useless than wax melted by the flame? So it is with the wicked, be they individuals or nations hostile to God (vv. 1, 2). This God has a tender care for the under-privileged individual (vv. 5, 6) as well as for Israel as a nation. At their head he had gone before them in the wilderness wanderings (vv. 7, 8) prior to settling them in the promised land (vv. 9, 10).

It is recorded that on these journeys the Ark preceded the people, and 'whenever the Ark set out, Moses said, "Arise, Lord, and may your enemies be scattered; may those hostile to you flee at your approach"' (Numbers 10:35). The virtual repetition of these words in verse 1 of our psalm makes a good introduction to the highly poetical description of the journeys and of the flight of nations before their advance (vv. 7–14); why should we be particular about a little poetic licence?

Zion comes into view where God loves to abide—so much greater than Bashan (Mount Hermon) with its three peaks (vv. 14, 15). God with his chariots has won the day, taking his captives with him—no rebel can live in his presence (vv. 17–23).

Triumphal entry

From battles long ago we are invited to watch the triumphal entry of God into his temple (vv. 29–31). Distant nations, Egyptians and Nubians (v. 31), look on amazed, bringing their tribute-gifts with them. We hear the singing. All are invited to 'make music to the Lord' (v. 32), to listen as 'he speaks in the mighty thunder' (v. 33). Israel's God has triumphed (vv. 34, 35). Right has won the day.

From our vantage-point of AD2000 we look back. We have heard of the rise and fall of the great world powers—Egypt and Babylon, Persia and Greece, Rome. We have lived through the crash of German domination. Some of us have seen the downfall of Pol Pot, Idi Amin, the South African apartheid regime. Smoke? Wax? Have we been watching the out-working of a divine principle, namely, that where there is iniquity there are the seeds of decay; that 'though the mills of God grind slowly, yet they grind exceeding small' (Longfellow); that human *hubris* and inflated arrogance will at last be humbled before the majesty of God's just rule? It is difficult for us mortals to get a philosophy of history which does justice to the facts. This psalm deserves a place in our thinking.

MEDITATION

So be it, Lord: thy throne shall never,
Like earth's proud empires, pass away;
Thy kingdom stands, and grows for ever,
Till all thy creatures own thy sway.

John Ellerton (1826–93)

How should we sing the above lines? As a declaration of faith,
as a prayer, as a thanksgiving—or as all three?

ZEAL *for* GOD'S HOUSE

Our psalmist is up to his neck in trouble. Nationally, it looks as if the cities of the country he loves need rebuilding—the people had been dispossessed. It may well be that he wrote as an exile in Babylon (v. 35). Personally, things could scarcely be worse. 'The muddy depths' (v. 2) remind us of Psalm 40:2. He is maligned by those who charge him with robbery; he asks helplessly, 'How can I restore what I have not stolen?' (v. 4). Part of the trouble is the outcome of his loyalty to God. He feels that that's a bit rough—'for *your* sake I have suffered reproach' (v. 7). 'Zeal for *your* house has consumed me; the insults aimed at *you* have landed on me' (v. 9). 'Life's hard', we hear him mutter. 'Why should it be the righteous who suffer?'

Part of the psalm consists of the words of malediction against his enemies upon whom he vents his wrath (vv. 22–28). The verses strike the imprecatory or cursing note which we have discussed earlier.

Some centuries later, a greater man of God than our psalmist was in Jerusalem, in the temple that the psalmist loved. He loved it, too. He grieved that a place designed for the worship of God should be so misused as to be turned into a market. In blazing anger he turned on the traders and the money-changers, upset the tables, scattered the coins. 'Take them out of here,' he said. 'Do not turn my Father's house into a market.' The disciples had never seen their Master like this. They recalled a line from one of their psalms: 'Zeal for your house will consume me' (John 2:12–17). The writer was our psalmist.

But all is not gloom and doom. Far from it. The psalmist turns to Jerusalem so far away. If he were there, he would join with the pilgrims and offer a young bull in sacrifice. But would that really please God? Here in exile he can offer something really acceptable to God— the thanksgiving of a loyal heart (vv. 29–31). This recalls part of the theme of Psalm 50:7ff. The thought comforts him and eases his pain. He can now even turn from his introspection and think of others. He finds himself addressing them: 'Take heart, you seekers after God, for the Lord listens... and does not despise his captive people', far though they be from Jerusalem and its temple worship (vv. 32–36).

As the psalmist recalls the goodness of God, the mud seems less sticky, the water less deep, the enemies less menacing. God reigns.

God saves. God listens. 'Let sky and earth praise him' (v. 34). He almost said: 'Hallelujah!'

MEDITATION

The fig tree has no buds,
the vines bear no harvest,
the olive crop fails,
the orchards yield no food,
the fold is bereft of its flock,
and there are no cattle in the stalls.
Even so I shall exult in the Lord
and rejoice in the God who saves me.

Habakkuk 3:17, 18

EMERGENCY CALL

The writer of this psalm is a man in a hurry—'make haste and save me' (v. 1); 'Come quickly... do not delay' (v. 5). It is an emergency cry. Unless God, who is his 'help and deliverer', comes to the rescue, he's had it! The man is a realist.

But precisely because he is a man in touch with God, he is also a man of hope. He sees the possibility of a day coming when his prayer will no longer be 'come quickly to my help' (v. 1) but it will be a triumphal cry 'All glory to God!' (v. 4). Put that in Christian terms, the Church *militant*, oppressed and battered, is also the Church *expectant*, and will be the Church *triumphant*. The progress is guaranteed, because the Church is founded on the crucified and risen Christ. The gates of hell will never prevail against it. It follows, as day follows night, that the Church militant and expectant is, in the here and now, the Church *jubilant* (v. 4). Or is it?

The signs of joy

Let us sketch a real-life situation. You have just moved house and gone to live in an area previously unknown to you. You have not been in the habit of going to church much, but you have been wondering whether this might be the occasion to join up with a local congregation and be part of a worshipping community. You decide not to hurry but to use the opening weeks in your new home to observe your neighbours. Before long you get to know who are the 'regulars', who the 'occasionals', and who never darken the church's door. You watch the regulars with special interest. At first glance there's not much to mark them out from the others. They go to the same shops, share the same problems, enjoy the same recreations as the rest. But as you look more closely, you *do* notice a difference. You find it difficult to put your finger on what it is.

Then you notice that there is about them an element which you can only describe as joy. I have avoided the word 'happiness', because somehow it is too shallow, too noisy, often too superficial. They do not make a parade of their religion, still less do they go down the street shouting 'hallelujah'. They do not try to 'target' you.

But there is an element about them hard to define. Our psalmist has done it for us. They are 'jubilant and rejoice in God' (v. 4). It is very attractive. It draws you to them. It might even draw you to God.

My sketch of a real-life situation is imaginary. But it poses a question: are we the Church jubilant? Do we live rejoicing in God?

PRAYER

Let hope keep you joyful;
in trouble stand firm;
persist in prayer.

Romans 12:12

PROCLAIMING *the* LORD'S WORKS

This is the psalm of an old man—and what a splendid old man he is! As is the way of old men, he tells us a good deal about his life, but without bragging. It has not been easy all the way, and he is not through the wood yet. He has suffered many grievous hardships and there are still menacing forces at work (v. 20). It would seem that he came from a godly home (vv. 6, 17). God has been, and still is, his rock and stronghold (v. 3), his hope, his trust (v. 5). Now he is old and his hair is grey (v. 18); he is conscious of failing powers (v. 9).

But don't run away with the idea that it is all over with him yet! Far from it. There is still work for him to do for the Lord who has been his God down the years. All his life he has proclaimed God's marvellous works (v. 17). He may not have much time left, but what there is of it he will use in magnifying his God. His eyes may not be as good as they were, but they are on the future: 'I *shall* praise you again and yet again' (v. 14); 'I *shall* declare your vindicating power' (v. 15); 'I *shall* come declaring your mighty acts' (v. 16). There is still work to be done; he wants to extol God's power 'to generations yet to come' (v. 18) and—here the old man gets a bit lyrical—'to highest heaven' (v. 19). Words fail him—he 'lacks the skill to recount' God's saving acts (v. 15). But while he has breath, he will speak. Then, with a kind of loving daring, he looks up into the face of God: 'Who is there like you, my God?' (v. 19).

A touch of glory

God has the power to revive even an old man and to lift him from the 'watery depths' of depression (v. 20). Then, though his fingers are stiff, out with the harp and lyre! Then, though the voice is a bit croaky, he will sing songs of joy, 'because you have redeemed me' (vv. 22, 23).

This is old age with a touch of glory to it. The psalmist is 'like a tree planted beside water channels; it yields its fruit in season and its foliage never fades' (Psalm 1:3). It still 'bears fruit in old age… luxuriant, widespreading trees' (Psalm 92:14). He ends his days proclaiming God's praises, witnessing to his Lord. Who is to doubt that all the trumpets sounded for him on the other side as he crossed the last river?

PRAYER

Lord God,
the protector of all who trust in you,
without whom nothing is strong, nothing is holy:
increase and multiply upon us your mercy,
that you being our ruler and guide,
we may so pass through things temporal
that we finally lose not the things eternal.
Grant this, heavenly Father,
for the sake of Jesus Christ our Lord.

Collect for Pentecost 14, *Alternative Service Book 1980*

The USE *of* POWER

This is another of the 'royal' psalms belonging with others such as Psalm 20.

In the days in which the psalmist lived, great power and authority lay in the hands of the king himself. Many of the functions which belonged to him have now passed to the State, to Parliament and its agencies. But there is much in this psalm which indicates how power—whether that of the Sovereign or of Parliament—should be exercised. These directions are timeless.

The psalm mentions God's justice and righteousness (vv. 1, 7); care for the underdog, the oppressed and the needy (vv. 4, 12–14); the fear of God, that is to say, reverence for him and obedience to his ways (v. 5). Put these things at the head of a nation's agenda and the nation will be great. Forget them, and the rot will set in. Then we can only cry for mercy.

> *For heathen heart that puts her trust*
> *In reeking tube and iron shard,*
> *All valiant dust that builds on dust,*
> *And, guarding, calls not thee to guard,*
> *For frantic boast and foolish word—*
> *Thy mercy on thy people, Lord!* (Rudyard Kipling,1865–1936)

In the Prayer Book of 1662 and in the Revised Book of 1928, ample provision was made in the services of the Church of England for prayer 'for the King's Majesty, for the King and all in authority under him, for the Royal Family, and for the High Court of Parliament'. These prayers were very frequently used. Since the appearance of the Alternative Service Book 1980, and since more and more people are entrusted with the leading of intercessions (both are things which I welcome), it is noticeable that the Sovereign, the Royal Family and the Government are less regularly prayed for. This is much to be regretted. The pressures put on public figures by the media and by the temptations of high office, often prove to be almost intolerable. That the Church should pray for such people is of paramount importance.

I write as an Anglican and in doing so have referred to the Prayer Books which we most frequently use. But whatever our denomination, the point which I am making applies. We are citizens. We are Christians. As such, we are people of prayer and people of action. We should constantly pray for those who exercise authority in our country; and we should play our part in implementing their decisions when they are consonant with Christian principles, and opposing them when they are not.

For MEDITATION

… I urge that petitions, prayers, intercessions, and thanksgivings be offered for everyone, for sovereigns and for all in high office so that we may lead a tranquil and quiet life, free to practise our religion with dignity. Such prayer is right, and approved by God our Saviour.

1 Timothy 2:1–3

Happy is the nation whose God is the Lord

Psalm 33:12

NOTES

NOTES

NOTES

NOTES

NOTES

NOTES

NOTES

NOTES

NOTES

NOTES

NOTES

PSALMS 1–72

THE PEOPLE'S BIBLE COMMENTARY

VOUCHER SCHEME

The People's Bible Commentary (PBC) provides a range of readable, accessible commentaries that will grow into a library covering the whole Bible.

To help you build your PBC library, we have a voucher scheme that works as follows: a voucher is printed on the last page of each People's Bible Commentary volume (as above). These vouchers count towards free copies of other books in the series.

For every four purchases of PBC volumes you are entitled to a further volume FREE.

Please find the coupon for the PBC voucher scheme overleaf.

All you need do:

- Cut out the vouchers from the last page of the PBCs you have purchased and attach them to the coupon.

- Complete your name and address details, and indicate your choice of free book from the list on the coupon.

- Take the coupon to your local Christian bookshop who will exchange it for your free PBC book; or send the coupon straight to BRF who will send you your free book direct. Please allow 28 days for delivery.

Please note that PBC volumes provided under the voucher scheme are subject to availability. If your first choice is not available, you may be sent your second choice of book.

THE PEOPLE'S BIBLE COMMENTARY

VOUCHER SCHEME COUPON

TO BE COMPLETED BY THE CUSTOMER

My choice of free PBC volume is
(please indicate your first and
second choice, as all volumes are
supplied subject to availability):

- ❏ 1 and 2 Samuel
- ❏ Psalms 1—72
- ❏ Nahum–Malachi
- ❏ Mark
- ❏ Luke
- ❏ John
- ❏ 1 Corinthians
- ❏ Revelation

Name: . . . .

Address: . . . .

. . . .

Postcode: . . . .

TO BE COMPLETED BY THE BOOKSELLER

(Please complete the following.
Coupons redeemed will be
credited to your account for the value
of the book(s) supplied as indicated
above. Please note that only coupons
correctly completed with original
vouchers will be accepted for credit.):

Name: . . . .

Address: . . . .

. . . .

Postcode: . . . .

Account Number: . . . .

Completed coupons should be
sent to: BRF, PBC Voucher
Scheme, Peter's Way, Sandy Lane
West, OXFORD OX4 5HG

Tel 01865 748227
Fax 01865 773150
Registered Charity No. 233280

THIS OFFER IS AVAILABLE IN THE UK ONLY
PLEASE NOTE: ALL VOUCHERS ATTACHED TO THIS COUPON MUST BE ORIGINAL COPIES.